LUCKY PEACH

A QUARTERLY JOURNAL OF FOOD AND WRITING

Peter Meehan
EDITORIAL DIRECTOR

Chris Ying
EDITOR-IN-CHIEF

David Chang
EDITOR

Rachel Khong
SENIOR EDITOR

Devin Washburn
ART DIRECTOR

Joanna Sciarrino
MANAGING EDITOR

Aralyn Beaumont
RESEARCH EDITOR

Ryan Healey
ASSOCIATE WEB EDITOR

Rob Engvall
JUNIOR DESIGNER

Emily Johnson
EDITORIAL ASSISTANT

Brette Warshaw
CHIEF OPERATING OFFICER

Priya Krishna
MARKETING MANAGER

Ethan Chandler
CIRCULATION SPECIALIST

CONTRIBUTORS
Gabriele Stabile
(Italian Photographer)

Mark Ibold
(SE Penn. Correspondent)

SPECIAL THANKS TO
Sascha Bos, Nikkie Bertrand, Kathline Chery, Jena Derman, Maddie Edgar, Ashley Goldsmith, Mary-Frances Heck, Michael Paul Light, C.B. Owens, Jeffrey "Jeef" Sobieraj, Lily Starbuck, Lucas Turner

HELPING HANDS
Suzi An, Tina Battock, Thai Chang-thong, Noelle Cornelio, Michelle Curb, Alexandra Forbes, Tanya Holland, Eli Horowitz, Joseph Johnson, Stephen Kent, Francesca Maniace, Camryn Mothersbaugh, Grace Nguyen, Rebecca Palkovics, Meghan Patke, Melissa Pinch, Philip Pinch, Paul Qui, Julia Rodrigues, Chad Robertson, Marya Spence, Sheri Warshaw

COVER ART BY **Jack Sachs**

READ MORE AND SUBSCRIBE AT

LUCKYPEACH.COM

ALWAYS UPDATED AND UP-TO-DATE
MADE OUT OF PIXELS INSTEAD OF PAPER

Letters, submissions, pizza, pies, pizza pies, etc. will find us at either of the below addresses

128 Lafayette Street,
Suite 302,
New York, NY 10013

12 Geary Street,
Suite 207,
San Francisco, CA 94108

Lucky Peach (USPS 12438) is published quarterly in Spring, Summer, Fall, and Winter by Lucky Peach LLC, 128 Lafayette St., Suite 302, New York, NY 10013. Periodicals postage paid at New York, NY and additional mailing offices. POSTMASTER: send address changes to Lucky Peach, PO Box 433324 Palm Coast, FL 32143-9559.

CanadaPost customer number 42740020.

Printed by RR Donnelley in Liberty, MO.

© Copyright 2016 Lucky Peach and the individual contributors.

Logotype above by Daniel Clowes

Original Lucky Peach logotype by Brian McMullen

Have you ever Snapchatted? Wanna Snapchat with us? Scan this code and let's be friends ;)

ADVERTISING INQUIRIES: ads@lky.ph
PRESS INQUIRIES: press@lky.ph
CUSTOMER SERVICE: 877-292-1504
or 386-246-0565 (outside the U.S.)

Editor's Note

It has been four and a half years since we launched *Lucky Peach* magazine (2,700-plus pages of stories and pictures so far), and a year since *luckypeach.com* went online (600-plus daily features).

We've got two whole books of new material done (*101 Easy Asian Recipes* is in stores now; *The Wurst of Lucky Peach,* our sausage compendium, goes on sale in April) and two more that will be done soon. There have been countless extracurricular adventures in making shit, like co-hosting the MAD conference in Copenhagen or bringing a fake restaurant to life or creating a weekly e-mail newsletter, that represent hours and hours of people's lives.

When people casually ask, "How's it going?" about *Lucky Peach,* my answer is usually "good." Because it is. We've done a lot of cool and stupid things that we (and our contributors) couldn't have done or done the same way elsewhere. We've built up a readership, both on paper and in pixels, at a time when there is a seemingly infinite number of other things one could choose to pay attention to. It would be shortsighted not to feel #blessed by the fact that good people (like you!) choose to read us.

But to say it hasn't been a struggle would be a lie. Money is hard to make. Circulation—

the business of printing and selling magazines—is a structure more archaic and possibly less hygienic than the bathrooms in *Game of Thrones*. The metrics that businesses like ours are measured by change weekly, and sometimes it's hard for us to internally agree about what's best. This is the tension of any for-profit creative endeavor, though: how to make the thing you want to make and make money; how to make the thing you want to make make money. We're doing our best.

Honestly, when it comes to pulling all this off, there's a lot of commiseration and collaboration between our two offices in San Francisco and New York, but we tried on the boxing gloves for your entertainment in this issue. This issue is all about conflict, and we explored a few other topics in this vein, working out my high-school-level understanding of the classic oppositional framework of stories through the ages— Man vs. Self, Man vs. Nature.

A final note: we were sad-

dened by the departure of devious burrito fiend and art director Walter Green at the end of the last issue—he'd been with us since the beginning— but now we have Devin Washburn wearing the chief art beret, and Rob Engvall in the drawing-stuff pocket, too. You'll notice they've moved the furniture around a little bit, hopefully to your liking. If not, we're happy to take this conversation outside: this is the Versus Issue, after all.

—PFM

THE LUCKY PEACH ATLAS

Brooklyn might be in Kings County, but everybody knows it's Queens that reigns supreme when it comes to eating in New York.

I'm not talking about those places with filament bulbs in the dining room and all the other garbage hipster trappings that will get a spot Bib Gourmanded just so the tire guys don't look over-the-hill. Queens is where a dozen dozen languages are spoken, largely by people without trust funds, maybe with families elsewhere catching a little bit off the top of the paychecks their loved ones earn making New York work.

Explaining what makes Queens such a great place to eat is a conversation that's longer than a ride from one end of the 7 train to the other. But for the sake of illustration, let's say you just ate at Donovan's Pub. (We'll pretend like you know the dark coziness that is Donovan's, the meaty majesty of its pub burger, the working-class-folks-having-a-nice-night-out vibe that makes the room a little electric. Because that's New York right there, great New York, the kind of New York that'll be gone someday or maybe it won't, but you can't help but feel that it has the kind of magic that money likes to push out and replace with a fucking Bareburger or something.) You've just taken down a burger and a pint or two, and you've got to take a walk to let the body do its work. You'll notice, in the blocks right around there under the train,

that it's real Irish, with brogues, blood pudding in the butcher shop, and people eating as though vegetables don't exist.

And then you walk a few blocks—just a few, not even a train ride's worth—and things are different: the red hair and freckles give way to somebody else's scene. Maybe you are in front of a Filipino bakery, where the Tagalog gossip pauses only long enough for a clerk to help you procure the sponge cake you're asking for, or maybe you're in a Thai grocery, ogling bottles and brands of fish sauce you've never seen before.

Or maybe you're like Matthew Volz, our artist friend from Queens, who's got an alfajor in one hand, watching it all go by under the rumble of the train tracks. I first saw Volz's drawings staring out at me from the cover of a record called Spit in the Face of People Who Don't Want to Be Cool, by the Beets, undeniably New York's finest Uruguayan-inflected garage rock band ever. Matt's best friend and regular co-conspirator is Juan Wauters—the leader of the Beets, who's now done a couple of solo records, both worth owning—who was his entrée into the Uruguayan community in Queens. And now Matt is your yerba-maté sherpa, a guy who can hip you to the heart of one of the seemingly endless number of scenes that makes Queens one of those food places nobody can step to. —PFM

COMIC BY MATTHEW VOLZ

IN THE SUPERMAN COMICS THERE'S A BOTTLE HE KEEPS SAFE IN HIS FORTRESS
OF SOLITUDE. IN THE BOTTLE IS THE CAPITAL CITY OF KRYPTON, A
CITY CALLED KANDOR, AND ALL ITS INHABITANTS SHRUNK DOWN TO
MINIATURE SIZE. EVERY SO OFTEN SUPERMAN SHRINKS HIMSELF DOWN
AND VISITS HIS OLD HOMETOWN. TO A URUGUAYAN LIVING IN NEW YORK,
37TH AVENUE FROM 84TH TO 87TH STREETS IN JACKSON HEIGHTS, QUEENS, IS A LOT
LIKE KANDOR—A PLACE WHERE YOU CAN TEMPORARILY SHRINK YOURSELF
DOWN, AND GO HOME AGAIN.

ON 85TH AND 37TH AVENUE THERE'S A PLACE CALLED LA GRAN URUGUAYA. INSIDE YOU'll FIND ALL KINDS OF URUGUAYAN SPECIALTIES: A HUGE SELECTION OF PASTRIES FILLED WITH DULCE DE LECHE, AND OTHER TRADITIONAL SANDWICHES AND BAKED TREATS. OLDER MEN SIT, TALK, DRINK COFFEE, AND WATCH SOCCER GAMES. THERE'S A BIG BELL HANGING OVER THE REGISTER THAT THE CASHIER RINGS ANYTIME THERE'S A GOAL. A GOOD MOVE IS GETTING A CAFÉ CON LECHE, AN ALFAJOR, AN EMPANADA, AND GRABBING A WINDOW SEAT FACING THE STREET. BLOCK-FOR-BLOCK JACKSON HEIGHTS IS ONE OF THE MOST ETHNICALLY AND CULTURALLY DIVERSE NEIGHBORHOODS IN THE WORLD. SO THERE'S SURE TO BE A TON OF WEIRDOS FROM All OVER THE PLANET FOR YOU TO TAKE IN WHILE YOU EAT!

LA GRAN URUGUAYA WILL ALSO HAVE EVERYTHING FOR ALL YOUR MATÉ-
DRINKING NEEDS. YERBA MATÉ IS NATIVE TO SOUTH AMERICA, AND
IS DRUNK FROM A GOURD WITH A METAL STRAW THAT FILTERS THE
HOT WATER THROUGH THE LEAVES. ITS EFFECTS ARE SIMILAR TO COFFEE,
BUT THE BUZZ ISN'T JITTERY. THE BUZZ KIND OF SNEAKS UP ON YOU,
AND YOU CAN EASILY LOSE TRACK OF HOW LONG YOU'VE BEEN AWAKE, THAT
STRANGE TERRITORY WHERE SIX P.M. AND SIX A.M. BECOME SORT OF RELATIVE.

ON 84TH STREET AND 37TH AVENUE THERE'S A PLACE CALLED EL CHIVITO D'ORO WHERE YOU CAN GET URUGUAYAN—STYLE ASADO. IN URUGUAY THERE ARE MORE COWS THAN PEOPLE (THREE COWS PER PERSON) SO THEY TAKE THEIR MEAT VERY SERIOUSLY! THE SIGNATURE URUGUAYAN SANDWICH IS CALLED THE CHIVITO, AND IT'S INSANE! IT CONSISTS OF HAM, A FRIED EGG, MOZZARELLA, TOMATOES, OLIVES, MAYO, AND LOMO (BEEF TENDERLOIN), SERVED ON A ROLL SERVED WITH FRIES. I HAVE NO DOUBT IN MY MIND THAT IF THIS SANDWICH WERE MORE WIDELY KNOWN, IT WOULD BE THE MOST REQUESTED LAST MEAL AMONG DEATH-ROW INMATES.

THE HEART OF THIS URUGUAY-IN-A-BOTTLE IS ON 86TH STREET BETWEEN 37TH AVE AND ROOSEVELT AVENUES. IT'S THE BACKYARD OF MY URUGUAYAN FRIEND JUAN'S PARENTS' BASEMENT APARTMENT. ON DAYS WHEN URUGUAY IS PLAYING A BIG GAME YOU'LL FIND JUAN'S DAD GRILLING CHORIZO, BLOOD SAUSAGE, PROVOLONE, AND STEAK, WHILE HIS MOM PASSES OUT SWEETS FILLED WITH DULCE DE LECHE. FRIENDS AND FAMILY DROP BY AND JUAN'S BROTHER DRAGS OUT THE TV AND CABLE BOX. THEY SET IT UP WITH EXTENSION CORDS RUNNING FROM THE HOUSE. WHEN IT'S ALL SET UP IT CREATES THE PERECT MIX OF FOOD, DRINKS, FRIENDS, AND SOCCER. IT'S AN EASY PLACE TO GET COMFORTABLE — IT'S A LOT LIKE URUGUAY IN THAT WAY. THESE BACKYARD SESSIONS TEND TO GO PRETTY LATE, AND LITTLE BY LITTLE EVERYONE HEADS BACK TO THE REAL WORLD. IF YOU DECIDE TO STAY LATE AND END UP BEING THE LAST TO LEAVE, YOU MAY HAVE TO HELP JUAN'S BROTHER DRAG THE TV BACK INSIDE.

CHEF VS. CHEF

Christina Tosi pulls back the curtain on TV cooking competitions

Each episode of *MasterChef* (and *MasterChef Junior*) pits amateur cooks against one another in one of several challenge formats: mystery box challenges (contestants all cook using the same surprise ingredient); elimination tests (loser goes home); team challenges (two teams compete for immunity from elimination); and pressure tests (someone from the losing team goes home). Milk Bar's Christina Tosi joined the *MasterChef* and *MasterChef Junior* judging teams last year, rounding out a judging panel of Gordon Ramsay and Graham Elliot, who has since left.

CHRISTINA TOSI: One thing I want to say right off the bat: there is *so* much footage that gets cut! Don't get mad that we didn't spend enough time with John Doe, that we didn't *all* taste his food, or that it looks like we told Jane Doe when to take her soufflé out of the oven but didn't give John Doe pointers, too. We did! We're probably the most fair people in the world—it just didn't make the cut, because we weren't interesting enough when we said it (or my hair was out of place). We want everyone to succeed. There is a team of standards-and-practices officials who watch the contestants' every move. Everyone has the exact same advantages, and we want them to leverage those advantages fairly.

LP: Thanks for that. The million-dollar question: Is Gordon Ramsay an asshole, or is that a feature he can turn on and off?

CT: Gordon is many things. He's hilarious and knows how to get anyone to crack a smile, he's an incredible businessman, and he's also a chef. A chef that grew under many great chefs, including Marco Pierre White! So yes, he can also be intense, and turn a seemingly harmless mistake in the kitchen into a *very serious affair*—and he's usually right when he does it. Part of the reason he became a great chef is because he grew up in kitchens where "asshole" wasn't a comment about a chef, but may very well have been a sentiment if you were that shortsighted of a cook or onlooker.

LP: Do you have to be more polite or diplomatic in your role as a judge than you do as a chef?

CT: If anything, I'd say in the first season of *MasterChef,* I was far less polite than my mother ever raised me to be (sorry, Mom!). The real talk is that I'm a girl and a pastry chef, plus I'm wearing a little dress and am all dolled up. The cooks aren't sure what to make of it ("If I flirt with her, will she vote for me?" Gross. No.). Some of the lovely folks on the other side of the TV at home aren't sure what to make of it either ("A leggy lady-boss? I'm not so sure about this..." Really, guys? Get used to it.) And so I did what I always do in situations like this—though I'm usually wearing jeans and a pair of high-tops—I get tough, and I don't give much away until I'm ready, and then I convince people why I'm at where I'm at. I'm a perpetually positive mentor, and you'll see a *ton* more of that in the coming seasons as I get my footing; as I hopefully lose some of the bells and whistles of being a female judge, I can just be myself.

LP: How often do you have to wait for beauty shots and stuff to happen before you can taste the food? Or do contestants cook extra portions for cameras in addition to the plates expressly for you?

CT: Cooks rarely cook an extra dish for beauty shots. The challenges and timelines are just too tight, and there's romance in the one dish that either takes you to the top or may very well be your fall from grace. Preparing two dishes just complicates things and takes away from the focus of the competition. It's the spirit of leaving it all on the table, literally. No excuses.

Because every dish you see on TV looks, well, beautiful, there is always down time between "Time's Up!" and when we taste. And we don't taste all of the food at once, because you just can't taste twenty dishes at the same time while they're all still hot.

The second that time's up and we know there will be a lapse, we go directly to each cook's station and inspect each element so that nothing can be lost in the transition. Keep in mind that we taste food at each cook's station as they work, so we have a good idea of who's looking good, and who is going down in a ball of flames.

And while you might think a piece of meat is going to overcook or that pasta is going to congeal—and you'd want to blame the time lag for a dish's stumble—the failures in the kitchen rarely hinge on that level of detail.

LP: What is a behind-the-scenes procedural drag that the audience would never guess existed?

CT: It can take *hours* to get the cooks in and situated, introduce the challenge, and read the rules. In order to make sure the competitions are fair (and something we can film and air with a clear conscience), everyone needs to start with the same understanding of what the competition is, and we have to confirm they hear every detail of the challenge. Stress does strange things to people—so immediately after we have painstakingly gone through every single aspect of what we're shooting, they stop paying attention, or they can't remember where to stand, or they start before you say so.

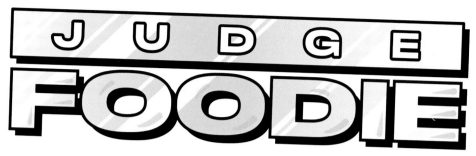

They think it's a steak challenge even though you said gnocchi. That does make for fun TV sometimes.

LP: Do you ever see people who are just totally lost? As in, do you ever give people a challenge and they get writer's block, but for cooking?

CT: Yeah, a lot. Or people will go in a direction they think is a great idea, and they'll realize halfway through it's a terrible idea—but it's also incredible to see how people recover. It happens more at the beginning than toward the end; at that point, they've been doing this day in and day out, so it's a muscle that they've built and strengthened. Never when someone is lost do they not produce something— and sometimes the best thing comes out of that. I think when you give yourself limitations, you actually end up being more creative; that fight-or-flight sense turns into fight, and I'm often amazed by how many clever things come out of people getting lost in a challenge. They're much more intentional, and they're much more realistic about what they can make happen with the amount of time they have to execute.

LP: Do you ever have dishes that are inedible? Or incredible?

CT: Very, very rarely inedible. I've never had someone mistake the salt for the sugar—that's the only way I could really see someone's dish being inedible. There are definitely plenty of things that don't pop and that aren't exciting or that just don't make sense—the most common thing would be too many things competing with each other on one plate.

I think, more than anything, the most memorable moments are the ones where you have a dish that's incredible. And I'll think to myself, *How did you do this in thirty minutes?* And it's not just making the dish delicious. We see the whole process, so you're also like, *How did you go from having no clue what you were making today, to being given rice as a challenge and making these amazing little rice pudding arancini balls?* And even as chefs, there are moments when something is so insanely delicious, we're caught off-guard, asking "You've never made this, you didn't know you were gonna make this, and you don't have a recipe?"

LP: Who are the bigger babies: *MasterChef* adults or *MasterChef* kids?

CT: The adults! They gave up so much to be on the show, they have *so* much riding on the opportunity, and as such, they have so much more to lose. It's much more intense. Adults are guarded and tricky. They are also the bigger babies. But we love them, all the same. **LP**

HOW TO OVEREAT PROFESSIONALLY

The various extremes to which competitive eaters push their bodies

By Emily Johnson
with Crazy Legs Conti, Major League Eater

THE BRAIN

Some gastroenterologists will tell you that humans actually have two brains. The enteric nervous system—the second brain—is a complex network of around 100 million neurons stretching from the esophagus to the anus. It sends signals to the brain in our heads via the vagus nerve and can control gut function independently of its upstairs companion. Competitive eaters must learn to fight messages of fullness and discomfort coming from the enteric brain.

Crazy Legs: It all starts with the brain. I have to have mind over stomach matter. I have to be zen. I have to center myself for an athletic event like any other athlete. I have to know my strategy going in. It is not so much me versus the food, as I am in it together with the food. I have to commune with the food.

POSTURE

An elongated stance, competitive eaters believe, better allows for the uninhibited passage of food through the digestive system.

Crazy Legs: I had always eaten low to the table, hunched over, and I'd always eaten tense, my whole body curved inward. But being upright, being open, is important while I'm really trying to get food up and down my throat, into my esophagus, and into my stomach.

THE MOUTH

Competitive eaters puff their cheeks out to store food before it is gulped down the esophagus—a technique known in the biz as "chipmunking."

Crazy Legs: I was actually told by the person I think is the best competitive eater in the world, Eric "Badlands" Booker, that the amount you can fit in your mouth is the amount you need to eat at every moment of the contest, which is a simple concept to think about. There is no tasting the food. Taste and other sensory things just get turned off.

ESOPHAGEAL MATTERS

At the top of the esophagus is the upper esophageal sphincter, a band of muscle that prevents food and liquid from entering the windpipe. Relaxing it (i.e., overcoming the gag reflex) allows competitive eaters to cram more food down their throats. The lower esophageal sphincter regulates entry into and out of the stomach, preventing stomach acid from escaping. Competitive eaters try to relax this involuntary reaction, enduring a little heartburn for the sake of victory. Crazy Legs uses warm water mixed with the sweat of an athlete he admires to loosen things up. (In the past he ordered sweat online, but now feels the marketplace can't be trusted, so he relies on "word of mouth through channels [he] would rather not mention. Nothing illegal, mind you.")

Crazy Legs: I use warm liquid because it loosens up the internal sphincters—all the sphincters except one, there's one that you really don't want to loosen. I have worn one adult diaper. It wasn't used during the contest, thankfully, but it could've come into play.

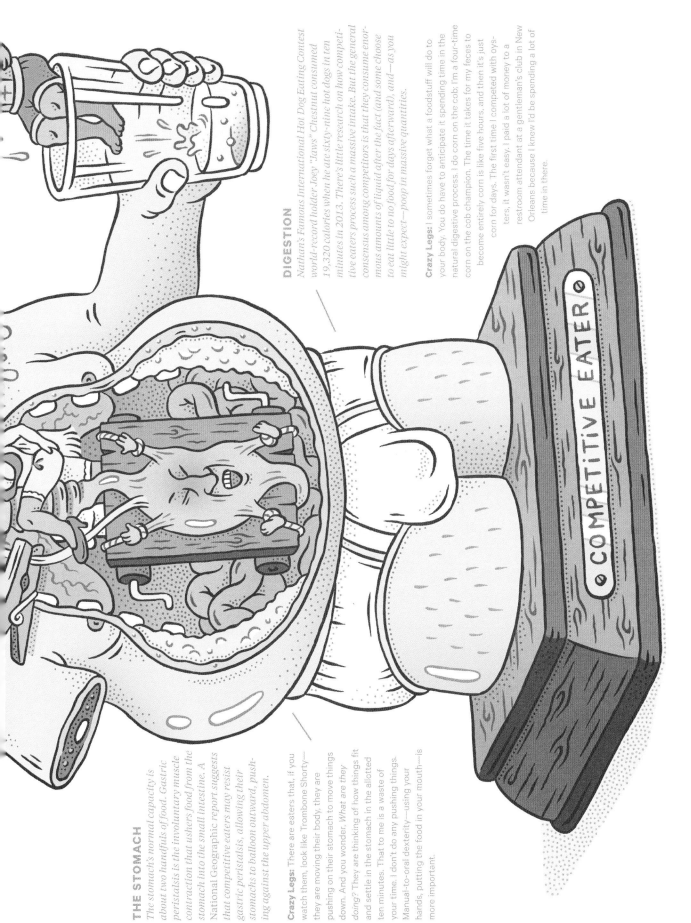

THE STOMACH

The stomach's normal capacity is about two handfuls of food. Gastric peristalsis is the involuntary muscle contraction that ushers food from the stomach into the small intestine. A National Geographic report suggests that competitive eaters may resist gastric peristalsis, allowing their stomachs to balloon outward, pushing against the upper abdomen.

Crazy Legs: There are eaters that, if you watch them, look like Trombone Shorty—they are moving their body, they are pushing on their stomach to move things down. And you wonder, *What are they doing?* They are thinking of how things fit and settle in the stomach in the allotted ten minutes. That to me is a waste of your time. I don't do any pushing things. Manual-to-oral dexterity—using your hands, putting the food in your mouth—is more important.

DIGESTION

Nathan's Famous International Hot Dog Eating Contest world-record holder Joey "Jaws" Chestnut consumed 19,320 calories when he ate sixty-nine hot dogs in ten minutes in 2013. There's little research on how competitive eaters process such a massive intake. But the general consensus among competitors is that they consume enormous amounts of liquid after the fact (and some choose to eat little to no food for days afterward), and—as you might expect—poop in massive quantities.

Crazy Legs: I sometimes forget what a foodstuff will do to your body. You do have to anticipate it spending time in the natural digestive process. I do corn on the cob. I'm a four-time corn on the cob champion. The time it takes for my feces to become entirely corn is like five hours, and then it's just corn for days. The first time I competed with oysters, it wasn't easy. I paid a lot of money to a restroom attendant at a gentleman's club in New Orleans because I knew I'd be spending a lot of time in there.

ILLUSTRATION BY JULES LE BARAZER

CRAB VS. CRAB

Debating two Southern styles of communal crab cookery with chefs **John Besh** and **David Chang**

Illustration by Christian Schubert

Lucky Peach Referee: Mr. Chang hails from the great state of Virginia, where they steam crabs, and—

John Besh: Yeah, where we ship a lot of our crabs from New Orleans, right?

David Chang: Where we know how to cook 'em.

LP: —and Mr. Besh is here to represent the Crescent City and the even deeper Southern tradition of boiling crabs. Mr. Besh, what are the pleasures of the crab boil as it's done in your parts?

Chang: If I go first then it's gonna be like one of those rap battles, and he's not going to be able to go.

Besh: It's all about the ceremony. First you start with the big pot, then you add lots of onions, garlic, lemons, celery, some water, then your spices: a lot of bay leaves, a lot of black pepper, a lot of mustard seeds, a lot of coriander, and a ton of cayenne pepper and salt. And you let that come to a boil for fifteen, twenty minutes, just allowing the flavors to mix and mingle before adding in your potatoes and sausage, and then, of course, the crabs. Let that come up to a slight boil, and then you're just going to let it sit and simmer— sometimes for a good forty- five minutes. There's some- thing magical about the sweet- ness of the blue-crab meat, fresh from the salty marsh of the estuaries of southern Loui- siana, mixing and mingling with the salt and the spice. You're breaking the crabs apart and you're devouring them, mak- ing sure that you're saving all those beautiful tops—with all the juice and the fat and the glands in them—for stuffed crabs later. It's a social thing— you're not boiling crabs for yourself. You're bringing peo- ple together around this big table, rolling up your sleeves, having some killer ice-cold beer, and just having at these crabs. It's an adventure.

LP: And what do you see as the shortcomings of the Mary- land/Virginia/Chesapeake Bay style of steamed crabs?

Besh: The truth is, I really love what they do, and I get it. But I find a lot of times with the steaming, if you're not careful, you tend to overcook the crab really quick, without impart- ing a whole lot of flavor. The flavor's in the powder that's on the shells, it's all over your hands. It's still good and I still like that, but I love the cere- mony of creating the boil and then adding the crabs and just letting them simmer. The crab takes center stage and you have all these other things—mushrooms, shrimp, crawfish, sausage, potatoes, corn on the cob— and this warm-pot, slow- cooking, everything-coming- together situation. And the anticipation of sitting at that table: that's almost magical.

LP: Mr. Chang, are your crabs magical, like his are?

Chang: John, I love you, you know this. But I almost want to offer you a draw right now. I think you've lost and you don't even know it yet.

Besh: I think I just need to bring you down here and show you how it's done, son.

Chang: Sure, sure. But let me explain it first. I know there's a

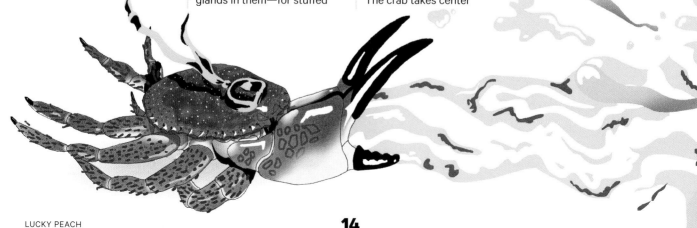

ceremony, and I'm not going to take that away from you. The crab boil is an amazing thing, as you say. But you also said something very key: the flavor is what's so important. So let's just focus on that.

I think that the flavor component gets lost when you boil crab—all the flavor goes into the water. Let's just say, instead of a crab boil, I'm doing a chicken boil with all that fuckin' awesome cayenne spice bullshit, and I throw like ten chickens in 'cause I got like ten buddies coming. We're each gonna get our own boiled chicken. Now, I wait my forty-five minutes, or however long until it's boiled to fucking shit—

Besh: What type of drug are you on right now?

Chang: I'm high on Old Bay. I just did an eight ball of Old Bay; my nostrils are a little flared up but it feels pretty good. That's another great way of using Chesapeake Bay spices.

Besh: If I were cooking a chicken, I also wouldn't put it in a steamer and douse it with Old Bay. That being said, add some chicken next time you do your crab boil and you're gonna absolutely love it. Some turkey necks—awesome.

Chang: Listen, I feel like Jack Nicholson in *A Few Good Men*: you can't handle the truth. Because here's the reality—

Besh: I still haven't heard how oversteaming and drying out your crab is somehow better for your crabmeat, versus slowly cooking it in this flavorful broth—

Chang: See, I didn't know your crab boil could defy the rules of physics and thermodynamics: that when *you* boil crab, somehow the water doesn't penetrate and extract flavors from the crab, and that somehow it's reverse osmosis and the crab extracts the flavor from the boil. Me, I'm vehemently opposed to boiling anything. You don't boil food.

Besh: I don't know, because I've been in your restaurants,

and I've seen a lot of boiling pots on the stove.

Chang: Water. Noodles. And I think that's overrated, too. I love you, but I'm just telling you: I grew up eating this stuff.

Besh: Explain it to me, walk me through it. What are you doing?

Chang: You get a case of really cold light beer, open up six of them, pour them into a big pot. Put a bowl in there or maybe some potatoes to prevent the crabs from actually touching any liquid. Add an ungodly amount of Old Bay everywhere. Literally, everywhere. In my nose, in the pan, wherever. You bring it to a boil and wait twenty-five minutes, and that's it. It's a very simple thing. Who oversteams crabs? It seems a lot easier to overboil a crab than to oversteam a crab. There's very little waste. I feel like every time you pour a beer into the pot to steam, you should drink a beer in honor of that wasted beer.

Besh: I'm liking that part. I'm agreeing with that.

Chang: And you know what

I've always been tempted to do? Drink the fucking dregs of that crab-steam beer. This is where, without a doubt, you would win hands down. I would fucking walk away, I would give you Momofuku and I would go work at Caesars in Atlantic City. If you guys made a soup out of the liquid from a crab boil, then I would be like, *Yes, you win*. And if you don't, then I don't see how I lose. Otherwise, if the boil is so great, then why don't we just cook everything that way? Why don't we throw a whole ribeye in there, and just eat boiled ribeye?

Besh: These arguments that you're making don't really apply. I'll let you get away with it. It makes you sound good, however, you're speaking total fiction.

Chang: You know what, fiction is assuming that a crab boil is superior to a steamed crab. That is fiction. And I would rather live in a land of boiled fucking chickens than crab boils.

Besh: We're just going to have to settle this in person. 🔲

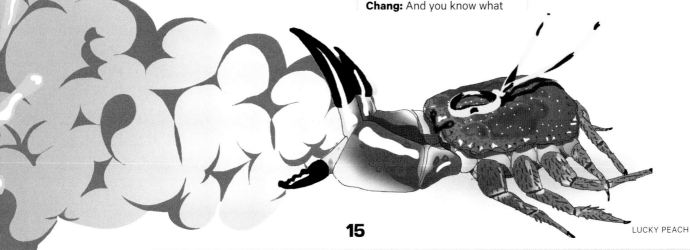

15

COFFEE OR TEA?

Asking a loaded question in Mumbai

By Michael Snyder   Illustrations by Dan Stafford

Tea is everywhere in India: in ramshackle roadside stalls; poured from big dull kettles by hawkers shouting garam chai!—"hot tea!"—on stifling, many-day train journeys; boiling away in grimy metal vats of milk; and sloshing over the tops of tall tapered glasses as it's rushed through the bazaars in handheld metal racks.

Even in the south, where locally grown coffee often takes pride of place in private homes, tea remains the everyman's drink. Probably the most powerful of Prime Minister Narendra Modi's populist bona fides is his oft-repeated story of a childhood spent vending chai: shorthand for humble beginnings.

But the opening of the first Café Coffee Day in 1996 (after India's economic liberalization), its subsequent expansion to an empire of 1,555 outlets across 219 towns and cities, and the more recent introduction of international brands like Starbucks have together consolidated coffee's image as the official beverage of global capital, and given it a decisive edge in the battle for the hearts and increasingly caffeinated minds of young, urban Indians.

Though India is the most prolific producer of black tea on earth, and the world's sixth-largest coffee grower, neither plant is indigenous, and until the early twentieth century, neither was commonly drunk (tea was brewed as medicine). In the early years, both crops were grown for export or for consumption by colonials on the ground, and were portrayed by the high-caste mandarins of Hindu cultural purity as dangerous foreign intoxicants. The British set up their first tea plantations in Assam in the mid-nineteenth century in order to fulfill their growing national demand and bypass the costly trade with China. Having captured nearly all of the British market by the early twentieth century, the Indian Tea Association, a trade group for planters, turned its attention to the population on its home turf, launching what one scholar, Lizzie Collingham, has described as perhaps "the first major marketing campaign in India."

To transform tea into a beverage of pleasure and leisure, the Indian Tea Association took cheap packets of tea and boiled them in sugary milk to suit the local palate. (Drinking spiced, boiled milk was a common practice.) They set up tea stalls at the mills and factories that drove the imperial economy, and dispatched tea vendors to railway stations across the country. Chai vendors would add local spices like ginger and cardamom to their brews to compensate for the low proportion of comparatively costly tea leaves. That

practice quickly became ubiquitous, and chai, the drink of India's working class, was born.

Coffee had been growing in India for at least a century when the British first set up their tea operations. According to legend, the first beans were smuggled into the sub-continent from the Yemeni port of Mocha by a sixteenth-century Sufi saint called Baba Budan, who was making his return journey from the hajj. The plants thrived in southwest India's tropical hills, and in 1760, Portuguese ships sailing from Goa to Rio de Janeiro carried one of the earliest coffee trees to Brazil, now the world's largest producer. By the 1920s, South Indian filter coffee—prepared as a slow, hot decoction, then mixed with boiled milk and sugar and poured back and forth between a pair of metal vessels to froth and cool—had become popular among the region's high-caste Brahmins. The coffee planters, however, never had the kind of cash that tea growers did to propagandize their crop, so its consumption remained local.

Coffee may be on the rise, but it still has a long way to go before unseating the reigning caffeine king. Last year India produced 2.6 billion pounds of tea, and consumed about two billion of those at home. India's coffee plantations turned out just 730 million pounds, and exported at least two-thirds of that. But while per-capita tea consumption hasn't increased in years, domestic coffee consumption has grown by 5 to 6 percent annually for a decade. Most of this growth is in instant, powdered coffee.

Brewed coffee—French press, drip, South Indian filter coffee, anything made from ground whole beans—is seen as too costly. And even with the emergence of several companies that source high-quality beans from Indian farms for sale to affluent, often globally connected urbanites in cities like Delhi, Mumbai, and Bangalore, coffee remains, for most consumers in India, more a matter of perception than of taste. Kunal Ross, who founded *theindianbean.com*, a retailer of single-source Indian coffee beans, told me one afternoon at a swanky café in my Mumbai neighborhood, "We're neither a coffee- *nor* a tea-drinking nation. We're a milk-drinking nation. Coffee and tea are just flavorings."

A few days after meeting Ross, I spent a scorching afternoon wandering between the corporate coffee chains that line a single three-hundred-and-fifty-meter stretch of road a short walk from my house. Recently, a couple of teahouses have set up shop in the same area, in keeping with the Indian Tea Association's goals of making tea competitive with coffee among young urban professionals. I spent the better part of two hours rudely disrupting conversations to ask: "Coffee or tea?"

At the local Starbucks (one of twenty-seven to open in Mumbai since 2012), where the staff screams "THANK YOU, BUH-BYE!" to every departing customer, I met a pair of young architecture students, one of whom told me, "Outside the house we drink coffee, but at home it's always tea." The other said her family serves coffee to guests, but otherwise drinks masala chai. At Café Coffee Day, a middle-aged real estate agent told me, "These joints are more about status." That evening I spoke with Harish Bijoor, a former vice president of marketing for Consolidated Coffee (now Tata Coffee) in Bangalore, who told me, "Every Tom, Dick, and Harish drinks tea. Coffee had to be discovered—it has romance."

Chai is still for laborers and gossiping aunties. Black tea is the effete drink of a faded empire. But coffee carries an intoxicating whiff of American capitalism, the great aspiration of India's unruly twenty-first century.

When you ask "Coffee or tea?" you're really asking a more important question: "Which world do you belong to?" **LP**

7 USES FOR A JUSTIN'S SQUEEZE PACK

(as told by Justin himself)

Portable
post-workout power

Liven up a
ripe banana

Hoard some in your desk
to avoid afternoon
tummy rumbles

Purse protein

Gift one to your hangry friend

Store a couple in your car
to keep the kiddos fed
during carpool

Pack it in your carry-on
for some much-needed
airport fuel

SINCERELY, *Justin*

sincerelyjustin.com

PERCEPTION VS. REALITY

With Harold McGee

Perception vs. reality is a venerable versus. From prisoners in Plato's cave mistaking shadows for reality, to studies about the unreliability of eyewitnesses, the difference between what is and what we perceive has been a problem for thousands of years.

When it comes to eating and drinking, most of us generally assume that what we taste and smell is what's there in the food. In fact it's not. Fortunately, the categorical accuracy of what is or isn't there is less important at the table than in the witness box. What actually matters at the table is perception. Perception is king when we're eating and enjoying. It is its own reality.

FLAVOR IS IN THE BRAIN, NOT IN FOODS

There's a simple fact that underlies the general discrepancy between perception and reality—why it is that we can't trust our faculties of perception to give us a full and straightforward account of what's around us: our brains and our senses are selective about what they notice about reality. They're error-prone, and each of us makes his or her own unconscious selections and errors. Each of us has perceptions that don't necessarily correspond to someone else's. These days, neuroscientists are telling us that flavor is all in the brain. Flavor is a perception, an experience that's constructed in the brain. Food is made up of molecules, and molecules by themselves don't have

any sensory qualities. Our experience of food is sensory: there's taste and smell and pungency, texture and temperature. The chemical and physical materials that generate these sensations in us do not, by themselves, have any of those qualities.

So the quality of saltiness is something that is the result of sensors in our tongue telling our brain that there are sodium and chloride ions in whatever we just put in our mouth. Our brain turns that into a sensation of *saltiness*. Yes, chemically, the food has salt in it—but the taste and experience of salt is a construction of our brain and the sensors that feed into it.

Moreover, each of us has a different set of sensors and a different brain. This is partly a matter of genetics. There are a half dozen taste receptors and a few hundred different smell receptors; no one gets a complete set, and everyone gets a different set. There can be a tenfold difference between one person and another in the number of taste buds on their tongues. And we all have different databases of experience to which the brain is always referring to make sense of what's going on in the moment.

The chili pepper offers another twist to the tangled nature of perception. You put something in your mouth and it is a certain objective temperature, X number of degrees Fahrenheit, and your body registers that particular temperature as being cold or warm or hot. Then you eat a chili pepper, and you eat exactly the same food at exactly the same temperature, and it seems hotter. Chili peppers contain capsaicin, a chemical that messes with the heat sensors on your tongue; it can shift your sensors' response by ten or fifteen degrees. Temperature is an objective, measurable thing, but our perception of temperature is very much dependent on our tongue, our brain, and whatever we may have exposed our temperature sensors to beforehand.

Smell is usually the dominant sense in the experience of flavor. The smell receptors in the upper nose report on some of the molecules that escape from food into the air, but when the brain turns that report into a smell perception, it edits it, taking into account past reports in its database of smell experiences. It's not a pure account of what smell molecules are present. Initially the brain is interested in a smell to evaluate what it might mean for survival. Is this stuff going to sustain me or kill me? Certain smells go with food, others go with danger, and so on. Your brain makes a prediction, and generates signals of attraction or disgust from the database it has accumulated.

When you think about how we describe tastes, we have abstract words for sweet and sour and bitter. But if you talk about aroma in a wine, it's going to be a leather saddle or a raspberry. We name smells by the materials we've experienced those molecules in before. The moment you smell something and recognize it, you're relying on past experiences of reality. Those experiences in turn influence what you experience in the moment.

•

MIXTURE SUPPRESSION

So flavor's all in the brain. But cooks create flavor by what they do with foods, even if in reality we're all experiencing things differently. They know that if you add salt to a food, you're going to increase everyone's perception of saltiness. Those things are commonsensical. But it can be useful for cooks to know things that aren't so obvious.

One is that some people are hypersensitive to salt, and others are hyposensitive. This isn't simply a matter of preference; it's the very different intensity experienced by different people from the same food. It's good for any cook to compare notes with others and know where his or her taste buds are on that spectrum. Salting only to your own taste can limit your food's appeal.

Another thing worth knowing about flavor perception is mixture suppression, which is how tastes and smells tend to dampen our perception of the other tastes and smells they are mixed with.

If you give someone a salt solution and ask them how salty it is, they might rate it a seven on a scale of ten. But if you add a little bit of sugar and ask them to rate the same solution again, they'll say five. The elements of a mixture tend to suppress each other.

Plainly, this means that if you really want people to experience something in particular, you actually don't want to have a lot of other stuff going on at the same time. If you have a very simple combination of tastes or smells, then you perceive those tastes and smells clearly. If you complicate the situation by adding more tastes or more smells, then your perception of the prior, already-there tastes and smells is diminished because now you've got something else to pay attention to. If you want to emphasize tartness, then you don't add salt or sugar, except if you want to balance it, in which case you are intentionally dampening down its perception.

You can think of mixture suppression as working a bit like an audio equalizer. With just one or two flavors, you have prominent peaks that are jumping way up above everything else. If you want to keep everything below the red line and balance and even things out, then you add a couple more components.

One notable exception to the phenomenon of mixture suppression is umami—glutamate and its coconspirators tend somehow to increase our sensitivity to salt. So if you add glutamate to something that's salty, it'll tend to taste saltier, not less salty.

Now, we only have a half dozen tastes that we know about, but we have thousands of different smells we recognize, so mixture suppression becomes more complicated with smell because it is much more various and variable.

There was an interesting experiment done by Dr. Noam Sobel at the Weizmann Institute of Science in Israel a few years ago that showed that if you mix enough different smells that are about equal in their intensity, once you have about thirty different odorants, you reach what he calls "olfactory white." It's kind of like white noise; you can't really pick out anything in particular. That's useful for a cook to keep in mind when composing dishes. Sometimes you just want to put all kinds of ingredients in there because they're cool, or they're interesting, or delicious in other contexts. But after a certain point you're just creating white noise.

There's also a limit to the number of smells that someone can actually distinguish and appreciate in a dish. Sensory psychologists have demonstrated that if you give people one familiar smell and then a second equally strong smell and a third and so on, the number at which they max out being able to identify the different smells is around four. Four!

Of course this was an academic exercise. When we're having wine or food, no one's engineered the experience to make sure every smell has an equal chance of being detected or not, and we take repeated sips and bites. Some flavors are stronger and some are weaker, some aromas fade while others persist. If you smell something that's really strong you may adapt to it, so the next sip or bite highlights something different. Still, when it comes to building the flavor of a dish, more isn't always more.

MULTISENSORY PERCEPTION

Our experience of flavor is influenced by other senses, not just taste and smell. Touch is how we judge texture, and vision and hearing also play important roles. Flavor is also affected by cognitive influences, by memories and thoughts and ideas about the particular foods that are in front of you.

Sometimes these non-gustatory influences are taken as evidence that our perceptions of food and drink are unreliable. Even wine experts describe the flavor of a white wine differently when a touch of red food coloring is added to it, and people have been known to like a wine more if it's described as expensive. Yes, our perceptions are easily manipulated. But the other way to look at it is, if you're aware of all these other influences on your perception,

as a cook or a restaurateur, you can use them to your advantage. Not to deceive or embarrass, but to intensify and enhance and emphasize. You can consider all the aspects of presentation and setting that influence the way people perceive what you actually put into the food itself.

Dr. Charles Spence is a sensory psychologist at Oxford who studies and writes extensively about these matters, which are called "crossmodal associations." He published a book in 2014 that I think a lot of cooks would be interested in, *The Perfect Meal: The Multisensory Science of Food and Dining*. It's a summary of the research that's been done on crossmodal correspondences with flavor: how the color of foods makes a difference to how we perceive them, as does the color of the plate, the shape of the plate, the music or noise in the background, what the menu or the server tells you about the food.

For example, in the early days of modernist cooking, Heston Blumenthal made a savory ice cream with crab at The Fat Duck. He discovered that if it was described as crab ice cream, people didn't like it much. But when he changed

the name to frozen crab bisque—exactly the same recipe—people loved it. That was higher-level thinking at work, affecting the basic perception and pleasure that we take in a food.

Sensory scientists have learned from experiments with brain imaging that if someone reads the word *cinnamon* on a menu, the parts of the brain that respond to smells light up. You're not actually eating or even looking at a fleck of cinnamon, but you're reading and thinking *cinnamon*, and that's enough to get your brain to be, in a way, virtually smelling cinnamon.

Dr. Spence's book is filled with dozens of examples of this kind. He and other researchers have found that in a setting where there are sounds that are not related at all to what you're eating, loud rock music or something like that, eaters tend to be less sensitive to the flavors in foods. They rate the foods that they're eating as being less intense and satisfying than they do if it's quiet, probably in part because they're less distracted and can actually sense more.

But sound can work in both directions. In a collaboration with Heston Blumen-

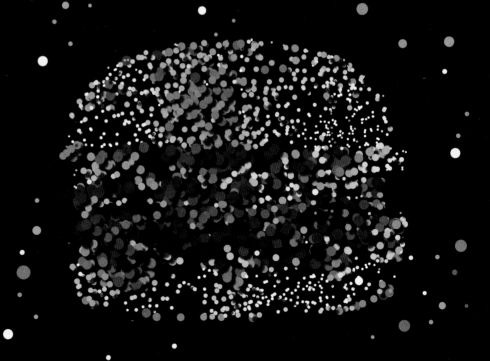

thal, Spence confirmed Blumenthal's hunch that if you supply noises that are somehow congruent to the experience of eating what you're eating, it has an enhancing effect on the experience rather than a distracting effect. That led to Blumenthal developing his dish "The Sound of the Sea," which looks like a line of seafoam on sand, has real sand visible underneath a glass plate, and is accompanied by a conch shell with earbuds through which you hear waves and seagulls.

Some establishments will be more interested in enhancing flavor perception, while others will be more interested in distracting from it. Work by Dr. Spence and others has shown that the noisier a restaurant or bar is, the less intense and less pleasant people perceive flavors to be—and the faster and more they tend to drink. Since a similar effect is seen in lab animals, it's been proposed that this effect is partly a stress response! So if what you're trying to do is sell drinks, it's a great idea to have loud music or lots of hard, noise-reflecting surfaces. And if you're like me and don't like loud restaurants, you can know that it's not just a matter of being unable to hear your companions. You're getting less enjoyment from the food, and paying for the privilege of subliminal stress.

PERCEPTION AT SECOND HAND

Knowing a bit about the realities of flavor perception can help any of us get more out of our perceptions. Because flavor is an experience formed in the brain, we can influence it by taking advantage of what some sensory psychologists have referred to as "perception at second hand." We can choose to open our brain to what other people experience or know—a story from a wine expert who chose the wine, or cheesemonger who chose the cheese, or impressions from our friends around the table. Our experience of that food or drink can be enriched by becoming aware of other dimensions that we might otherwise not have noticed.

We can also choose to make an awareness of how we perceive flavor part of the experience. That can encourage us to pay more attention to the details, to work a little harder to pin down qualities and echoes and resonances and personal meanings.

I realize that it probably sounds paralyzingly overwhelming and crazy to talk like this about something as basic as tasting food! But what it boils down to is: if you're aware of how your perception of flavor can be shaped by all these different factors, then your inner reality can be as rich and complicated as you want it to be. It's up to you to construct it. **LP**

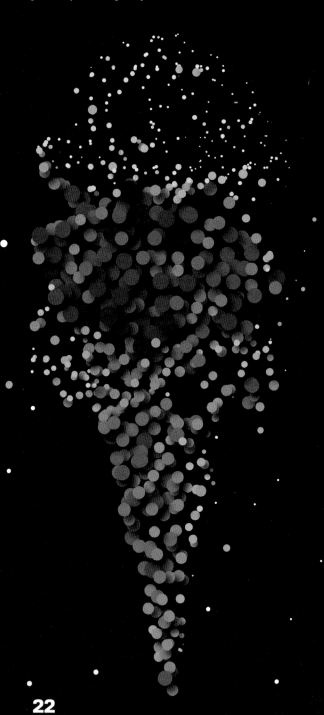

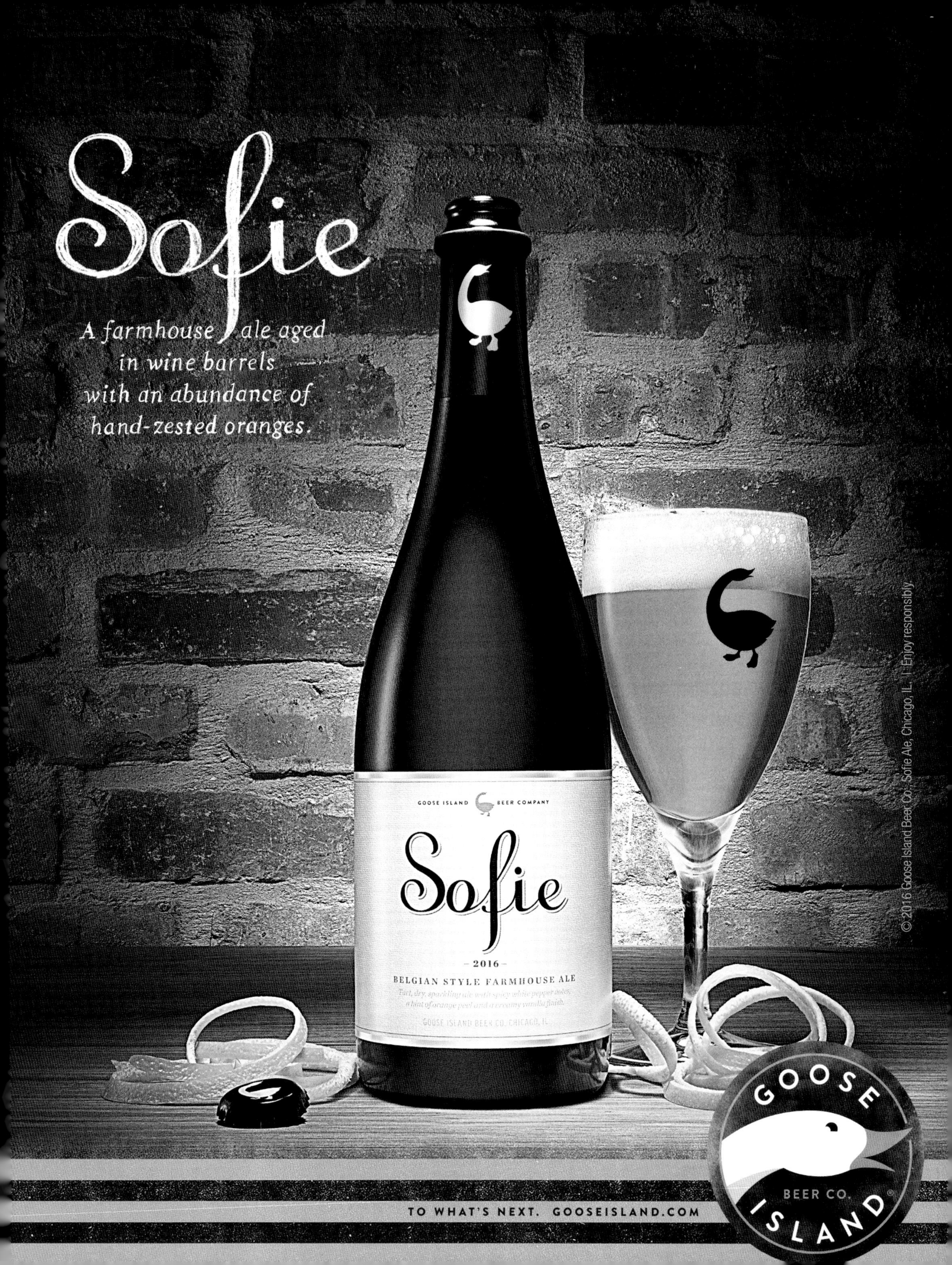

Sofie

A farmhouse ale aged in wine barrels — with an abundance of hand-zested oranges.

GOOSE ISLAND BEER COMPANY

Sofie

— 2016 —

BELGIAN STYLE FARMHOUSE ALE

Tart, dry, sparkling ale with spicy white pepper notes, a hint of orange peel and a creamy vanilla finish.

GOOSE ISLAND BEER CO. CHICAGO, IL

GOOSE ISLAND BEER CO.®

TO WHAT'S NEXT. GOOSEISLAND.COM

EDOUARDO JORDAN

Edouardo Jordan, the thirty-five-year-old chef and owner of the half-year-old Salare in Seattle's Ravenna neighborhood, wears braces on his huge grin. He flashes them often. We're drinking gin. He asks if I'll be okay tomorrow, and I assure him I will. "Most of my Asian friends can't last past one or two drinks," he says. "And you're like seventy-nine pounds, too." This is exactly what we're here to talk about. All of us have to go through life being who we are in our bodies—bodies we didn't pick out, but have to live with anyway.

I tell him I compensate for what I look like in specific ways that are hard to explain to someone who's bigger and a man. Getting people to take me seriously, for example, takes a lot of extra effort. Jordan knows something about this—about having to deal with the body you've got. As a black chef working in fine dining, he's an uncommon sight. His kitchen crew is mostly white; his restaurant's diners, too, are overwhelmingly white. Jordan's hair is cut short and neat, and he is, like I said, perpetually smiling. He's got a happy-guy, gentle-giant vibe. "If I had walked into the French Laundry with gold teeth and dreadlocks, they would have been like, *Fuck that*." —Rachel Khong

I'm from St. Petersburg, Florida. My family always cooked—Sunday suppers at my grandma's house, family reunions. I went to the University of Florida, and I'd cook in college for my girlfriends—girlfriends with an s—and for my boys, who'd say, "Damn, dude, you good." I was always cooking, all the time.

I ended up going to culinary school—Le Cordon Bleu in Orlando. I'd grown up eating and cooking Southern food—collard greens and chitlins, dirty rice, black beans, ham hocks, smoked turkey necks—really heavy, old-school Southern cooking. I knew that the only way I was going to get better at cooking was if I expanded my circle.

I was twenty-four, a little older than most kids in culinary school. I really took it seriously. In the end, I wished I'd spent that cash learning a different way, because I was so serious about it and everyone else was a jokester. But going to culinary school did open my eyes. I was in the library when I first opened the *French Laundry Cookbook*. I was like, *Damn, there is a lot more going on outside little Florida.*

I realized that the only way I was going to get better was if I worked with some of the best people in the country. I started applying for the French Laundry at that point—they never really returned my calls. I got a restaurant job in Tampa and kept sending my resumé to the French Laundry, and finally I was like, *Fuck it, I'm going to fly out there.* Me and my girlfriend at the time—she's now my wife—ate in San Francisco, hung out, went to Napa, and stopped

at the French Laundry. We couldn't afford to eat there, so we didn't go in, but I was waving out front. I met Devin Knell, who was the executive sous chef. He said, "Just send me your resumé and we'll talk." So I sent him my resumé, and four or five weeks later he e-mailed me and said, "Whenever you're ready to come out, come out." I was like, *Okay. Opportunity!*

After his apprenticeship at the French Laundry, Jordan took a job at the Herbfarm in Washington, where his wife is from and her family still lives. From there, he went to New York to work at Per Se, then followed chef Jonathan Benno to Lincoln Ristorante. Eventually he moved back to Washington for good, where he connected with Seattle chef Matt Dillon and wound up at Bar Sajor. He spent nearly three years as their chef de cuisine. Opening his own restaurant had always been the goal, and after applying for loan after loan, plus a Kickstarter, plus a lot of hands-on labor, Salare opened in June 2015.

It's been eleven years now, and I've worked with maybe five black chefs. I remember five black students in culinary school—there were a few more that I didn't personally know. One kid was from my hometown. He was good, he was a hardhead. He ended up cooking on an oil rig in Louisiana. After culinary school, you need a job that's going to pay the bills, because you have to pay back your loans. I think that's a struggle for those of us—often minorities—who don't come from a financial background where we're able to get put up a little bit by our parents. We can't forgo paying rent this month because we know Mom and Pop or whoever will take care of it.

My family wasn't necessarily poor, but we didn't have everything. We lost our house when I was fourteen. We were sleeping on my neighbor's couch for six months, sleeping on my grandmother's couch for another six months, and then

we finally found a house that we had to rebuild, my Pop and I.

They were and are very supportive of what I do, but I always knew that whatever I did, I'd have to do it on my own. I knew that I could never depend on them to get me out of a struggle or pay for culinary school. I didn't travel out of the country until I was twenty-six, so I was totally behind in the sense of learning about different foods and seeing different cultures. I always felt behind, and I had to work that much harder to catch up. Not from a skills standpoint—just understanding and seeing how food should be plated, how service should be. You miss that opportunity if you can't afford to go places. There are a lot of obstacles that are bigger than actually being in the kitchen and being able to perform.

My father was not educated at all—he's illiterate—so we suffered as a family, because there were things we couldn't do since we had to accommodate him. I personally knew I'd have a better life for myself—a better life for my family—in the long run than what I'd had. Nothing against my Pops, but I also wanted to be a bigger and better man than he was. It wasn't his fault. So I'm always trying to figure things out, I'm always working harder than the next person; I barely sleep. I always push harder than most people, and I'm still trying to do that now.

It hasn't been an easy road; there were times when I was like, *What the fuck am I doing? Why am I doing this?* I had probably my worst Thanksgiving ever working in Napa. I was alone with this old white lady eating canned cranberries and some white rice and a store-bought turkey. I was really homesick. I could've easily turned left or turned right and said, *Forget this,* but luckily I kept going. Napa was where I saw that caliber of food for the first time. That was a whole new world to me—the sense of urgency and perfection.

I didn't get yelled at a lot, but I did get

yelled at. I think people thought twice about truly yelling at me, because they didn't know how I was going to react. As a black guy, I was a new thing to them. *Am I going to yell at this guy, and is he going to throw a fucking pan at me?* A lot of chefs in restaurants don't hire black people because they don't know how to relate.

There was no special treatment for me in the kitchen. But I could see people holding their tongue a little more. I ride people a little bit harder in my kitchen than most. You have to get in people's heads. They didn't know how to get in my head. They didn't know who I was, where I was from, what I'd been through.

Seattle is not very diverse. I saw four African Americans in my restaurant tonight, and I made it a point to walk to that table and say hello and thank you. They actually came to my restaurant because they'd read an article about black culinary leaders in Seattle, and came in to

support me. And I really, really appreciated that. I knew they came for a reason. My restaurant's normally filled with Caucasian folks—not black folks.

Everything I cook is an expression of who I am, what I am, what I've seen, what I've tasted. When I was leaving Lincoln, Chef Benno said, "You've got to find your voice."

Well, finding a voice takes time. You can't go to culinary school and walk out and have a voice. You may have known for years what Mom and Pop cooked, but that's not a voice. You've got to learn fundamental skills—how to be fast, how to be persistent, how to be consistent, how to be clean. You have to earn your rights, earn your rank, and then from there you definitely have to figure out your cuisine— who you are. I tried to avoid being the black chef, the Southerner, the soul-food restaurant. I avoided that.

The black guy opens up a barbecue restaurant and that's what he's known for.

I didn't want to be that. One day? Yeah, I want to open up a barbecue restaurant. But I don't want that to be my first restaurant. I don't want that to be what people recognize me for.

I don't have fried chicken on my menu because I don't want to be the fried-chicken-and-waffle restaurant. That's what every black restaurant has on its menu. But I have takes on it: I did a confit duck leg that we deep-fried and served with quinoa and a duck-liver mousse. That's my take on fried chicken with collard greens. It's probably the best duck-liver mousse in the city.

I ask Jordan if he has black cooks in his own kitchen.

That's a sore subject for me. I actually had one black cook come to me. His mom introduced me to him, she was a loyal customer. I was like, *Fuck yeah. Young black cook who wants to learn.* Green. Great.

No problem. I'm going to be here for you. As long as you put your time and energy into me, I'm going to put my time and energy into you.

I thought, *Great, I can teach this guy. I can be a mentor to him.* But he was not committed. He didn't have the energy, and was definitely slower than everyone. I expected that: this is a whole different world and my kitchen is not the easiest kitchen—especially not in Seattle. I expect a lot and I ask a lot. And he was just moping around, didn't really ask me any questions, didn't show a sense of urgency, didn't really care. I was out one night after a long service, and I saw him walking the strip. He was due back the next morning at six a.m. He was the lowest-level cook in my restaurant, out at one thirty a.m., and supposed to be back at my restaurant working at six that morning. It clicked with me that he wasn't committed. I had to have a conversation with him. It kind of went sour. It sucked.

I know personally I have my heart and soul in this industry. Anyone I'm going to mentor better have their heart and soul in it, too. Because I'm putting my time, my energy, and my money into them, I expect more from them than what I actually put in or at least equal to what I do. He was the first person that I was able to take in, and I thought, *All right. This is my black culinary child.* Did not work out. And for my kitchen crew, who saw that and knew what I was doing, it put a bad taste in their mouths. It affected what they came to expect and think of the next black child who comes into the restaurant. *Is chef taking them in to mentor them? Is he going to give them special treatment? Who are they?* And that shouldn't be the case. They should fucking walk in just as hungry and eager as any other cook, no matter who they are. Woman, white man, purple man, fat man. Tough. I can't count all the white cooks I've forgotten who have come through my kitchen, but that one

black cook is going to be imprinted in my brain for life. There was my opportunity to mentor a young black cook. I wish I'd had that. Who knows where I would be now? I know the road could've been a little easier if I'd had someone to call to grab a beer with.

Name a black chef who's won an award besides Marcus Samuelsson. It's a celebrity show, culinary politics. I did a little research and I'm going through everything that I can possibly find, and there are maybe one or two minority chefs recognized by the James Beard Foundation a year, if that. It's pretty fucking sad. I want to have a say in this. I want to stir it up. But I don't know: Is that their problem or my problem? Or *our* problem? 🄻🄿

GABRIELA CÁMARA

Gabriela Cámara doesn't exhibit any of the guardedness or manic restlessness of so many other restaurateurs I've met. She opened her first restaurant, Contramar, eighteen years ago while studying art history in college in Mexico City. She never meant to be a chef or a tycoon; she simply wanted to open a place where she and her friends could eat fresh seafood.

Today, Contramar is a Mexico City institution. At lunchtime, a fleet of waiters in white dinner jackets and bowties darts around the dining room, ferrying tuna tostadas (their signature, oft-imitated dish) and large oval wooden platters with a whole fish splayed flat, one half covered in red chili, the other in bright green parsley salsa.

When I heard that Cámara was planning to open a spot in San Francisco, I balked at the idea that she'd be able to meet the staffing requirements of a restaurant like hers. Not here in San Francisco, where chefs joke morbidly about the dearth of capable, willing servers and the impossibility of finding enough people to work the floor.

My suspicions were seemingly confirmed when I had dinner at Cala, Cámara's tenth restaurant and first in the States. My waiter was earnest but unpolished. I told him my drink order, and watched as he struggled to translate what he'd heard into something he recognized on the menu. He asked me twice to clarify. Once he left, I mentioned it to my dining companions, who told me something I didn't know: a majority of Cala's staff comprises former drug addicts and ex-cons who have come through job-placement programs and halfway houses. It's not something they advertise—had my friends not told me, I'm sure that I would have eventually lost patience for our waiter's greenness.

For the next week, I couldn't get the restaurant and all of its inherent conflicts out of my head. Idealism versus practicality. San Francisco versus Mexico City. Good sense versus wild risk. The restaurant seems to embody these tensions. It's still young, and while it just received three and a half stars from the *San Francisco Chronicle*, it buzzes with possibility: it could still all go terribly wrong or magnificently right. —Chris Ying

Chris Ying: First off, Mexico City versus San Francisco.

Gabriela Cámara: Oh my god, two very different cities. Mexico City is humongous. San Francisco feels provincial next to Mexico City. On the other hand, I have come to learn that there are many very similar issues between San Francisco and D.F. Even though there is a larger middle class here, some people are just total outcasts from society and yet still live where everybody else lives. They are people that you sort of don't see. There is this whole part of society that nobody talks about, and I have come to find that very troubling about San Francisco. You don't think of the United States or of a rich city like San Francisco as having this terrible social structure, or cultural encounters between such different worlds. Mexico is all about these high contrasts.

CY: Why did you decide to open your restaurant here?

GC: The father of Lucas, my kid, wanted to live in San Francisco, so I said let's go. I have no attachment to San Francisco. It's a good thing for Lucas—he can learn English well, not be in Mexico City for a period of his life. Growing up as a privileged kid in Mexico City is, I think, terrible. I thought I might as well do something in San Francisco. And I know it's the worst city to open a restaurant in, and I knew it was going to be very difficult. I was chickening out of it until I found this amazing location. And then I found Emma Rosenbush, our general manager, who used to live in Mexico City and moved here because her boyfriend is making wine. She started

working with me, and then it just started happening.

CY: Is it easier to find cooks and waiters in Mexico City?

GC: I think it's difficult to open a good restaurant no matter where you are. But definitely the waitstaff in San Francisco, for me, was an issue, and this is why we went to the probation department.

In Mexico City, waiting on tables is a trade that people are proud of, a trade that people actually aspire to. Here, it's like you wait tables while you're studying, or while you're freelancing in another job that you're *actually* interested in. It's a way of making money when you're in college or whatever.

It's difficult to find good cooks anywhere. Really difficult. And good members of the staff? Really difficult. And my experience, in Mexico City, is that the only way you can have good staff is if they're involved in what you're doing, and their lives benefit from working with you. Like, it makes sense for them on more than just the economical level.

CY: What are the differences in your approach as a chef between Mexico City, where people understand what Mexican food is, and San Francisco, where we're just starting to understand more than tacos?

GC: In Mexico City, there was not one seafood restaurant that had really fresh seafood. They had these frozen, sort of elegant fish either from Europe or from Chile or Alaska, and the local fish was *huachinango,* red snapper. But the idea of a fresh piece of fish, just grilled and not covered in sauces and all these things, was really... nobody was doing it. So that was sort of new, in a way. The parallel I would find here is to make Mexican food that is not what the public is used to in this part of the world. It's not that I'm taking

advantage of people's ignorance, but I'm taking advantage of a hole, of a missing part of cuisine in a city where people are so obsessed with food.

CY: Both at Contramar and here, the service is a talking point. At Contramar because you've got all these well-appointed, white-jacketed servers running around, eight to a table or whatever the case may be, and—

GC: It seems that way, but they're actually so good that it just feels like that!

CY: And then here, service is a talking point because of where you're finding your staff and what you're doing for them. What is the thinking behind how you staff there? What's the thinking behind how you staff here?

GC: It's not that I started out wanting to do a social project. In Mexico, you have these outcasts of society who, through service in restaurants—basically serving people that have more money than them—can make a better living than by doing any other manual work. If they don't have a college degree or they don't have a good social position in terms of their families, it's a good profession to get into good money. What I've figured out is that it's best to have servers who really care about the place. And you can only have people who really care about the place if they make good money, and if they're held responsible for the diners' experiences. I pay the waiters much more than they would get paid anywhere else. Then there's profit sharing. For many years, workers' rights—not only in Mexico—were not considered. Until the minimum wage goes up to fifteen dollars, who's paying fifteen dollars? You don't want to do more than you need to. All these laws make us do only as much as we're required to. Not to make it like a hippie commune—it's not that they're

all partners in the business, but they are partners in the results. We've all made good money. I really believe that the distribution of capital is such a big issue in the world. If it were more evenly distributed, the world would be a better place. I do think that people who have money have to stop wanting more and more and more and more at the expense of others not having as much.

CY: Do your waiters and servers and staff at Contramar end up staying with you for a long time?

GC: Forever. Last year, a waiter that had been working with us for seventeen years retired. Almost everyone has been working with me for at least ten years. I mean, it always happens that you do have to hire new ones. When we opened the terrace, we needed five more waiters. But if you're a server and you live in Mexico City, you're lucky to work at Contramar.

CY: Here in San Francisco, I know it's not a charity, you're not running anything like that—

GC: No! Let me tell you how I came about this. I was always like, *Emma, so how are we going to get good waiters? I think the service in San Francisco is terrible.* Pretty much in most cases, it's bad. You go to places where waiters are telling you how they feel in terms of the food and the wine, and they're okay, and they're trying to do their best, but there isn't this service culture. I get it, your interests are as important as mine, but I'm not going to be servile to your interests. I get that it's a dignity issue. But on the other hand, I find that it's very dignified to do something well, and be paid well to do it. I love serving others. I love having people come to my house: cooking for them, serving them, showing them a great time. I don't mind opening wine bottles for them, and serving them

wine, and washing the dishes. I love that. So I think if you can make all your waitstaff have that attitude, the restaurant transforms into a place that is very welcoming. My issue was: *How the hell are we going to get people to wait on our guests in a more welcoming manner?* And Emma, who had worked at a prison law office, was like, *You know, there are all these ex-cons that can never find jobs. And the probation department has all these programs that want to help people get jobs. And people don't really have other chances, because most people don't want to deal with ex-cons.*

CY: You weren't hesitant? You thought this was a great idea?

GC: I laughed, and we joked about it, like, *Oh my god, we're gonna have all these characters.* But in Mexico, I've had all these characters. The whole crew of people who work for me are ex–drug addicts, ex–gang members, or they come from really fucked-up backgrounds. They get it together because they see an opportunity and they're inspired, and they get it together for themselves and for their families. You have no idea how much I've learned about alcohol and drug addiction, because I go through these programs with

them, and I take them to rehab. I've dealt with this. So I wasn't scandalized about going through the probation department. I was just curious as to how people would take it. I didn't want to use it as a publicity tool. I didn't want to be the Jamie Oliver of saving San Francisco society. I did not have that pretension.

CY: I love that the original reasoning for it was: *There are no servers, we can't find anybody. This is a workforce that is ready and available—why don't we use them?* You're approaching it from the practical side of things. But you've talked about this in the past: there are training difficulties to overcome with people who have never set foot in a restaurant like this—

GC: —and don't know the difference between sparkling and still water. This was one of the questions.

CY: Practically speaking, do you worry about recidivism and relapse? Is it a thing you have to worry about more with a staff that has addiction problems or has had previous records?

GC: Yeah, we do—we have dealt with it. But as with any restaurant, people come at the

beginning, and you have this crew of people that you recruit from different walks of life. You have job descriptions, and you think people meet the job descriptions. I have never opened a restaurant where you have 100 percent of your staff stay on after the first three months. In the first three months, around 30 to 40 percent of the staff rotates. Always. I mean, the probation department also helps you make sure that these people actually are okay; they go through all the applications. But this is also part of trusting in our society, because why would they be let out of jail if they can't be outside? So we have had rotation, we have had people not work out. Before we opened, a couple of guys didn't make it because they went back to jail. It happens no matter what. Even the cooks with the best credentials sometimes don't work out.

CY: Do you think about this kind of long-term picture, or is it just like, *Let's get through service today*?

GC: I hope it transforms their lives. If you are convicted in a federal prison, and then you get out and go to a halfway house, you may have to be close to where you were incarcerated. So some of these people are forced to be in San Francisco for a few years, but might eventually want to go back to their homes in the Central Valley or in Southern California or wherever—some of these people might leave and go be with their families in two years. I don't expect them to stay here. But for some of them, it has been a life-changing opportunity.

CY: Are other restaurateurs asking you about it?

GC: They are. I am hoping they go on to try this. I am hoping. Because everybody has such issues staffing. It is a disaster. My friends in New York are asking me about these programs. Getting good people for restaurants is an issue, always. **LP**

33

N
YORK
VER
SA
FRAN

ILLUSTRATIONS
BY SAM LYON

W

CITY
SUS
N
CISCO

Whose cuisine reigns supreme?

We pit the City by the Bay against Gotham in a food-on-food cage match. Many foods enter—sandwiches, samosas, salads, even some undisputedly famous yet terrible dishes—but only the most delicious stagger out intact. Who's got the best burritos? The best pizza? The best whatever?

Flip the page and dig in!

SUCCESS IS A JOB IN NEW YORK

By Peter Meehan

To argue the superiority of eating in New York over eating in San Francisco is to compare wildly mismatched fruits.

In one corner, there's the Big Apple, eight and a half million strong, an unruly, unrulable polytheistic polymath, the economic capital of the world, where the huddled masses unhuddle and turn into Americans—or, really, make America theirs. In the other corner, there's the self-important kumquat of a township called San Francisco, forty-seven square miles of drafty apartments that coders live in before they get tired of riding the Google bus and move down to Mountain View. In fact, to compare any municipality in the United States to New York is just a way of lying to yourself: your city doesn't compare.

This is okay, though. Having been in New York for almost twenty years now, I often pine for elsewhere. I lust for the diversity of Chinese cuisines to which the greater Los Angeles area can lay claim, and for the salty, beefy foods of my Chicago childhood. When I visit the Brooklyn Botanic Garden and walk into the Warm Temperate Pavilion, I am made weak in the knees by the perfume of piney trees and plants—the mix of rosemary, lavender, eucalyptus, and who knows what else (I'm a New Yorker, not a botanist) that seems to grow wild on every non-piss-covered street corner in San Francisco.

So here's the thing: I get it. Your city is nice. Maybe nobody steals your bike there, or your farmers' market doesn't turn into a brown-and-gray parade of root-cellar rejects for half of the calendar year. But your city, especially when your city is San Francisco, is no match for New York.

Oddly, the one place that I can't get out of my mind when I think about this matchup is Punjabi Grocery & Deli, a subterranean cabstand on First Street near Avenue A, on the border between the East Village and the Lower East Side. All the food is vegetarian, prepared at a mothership location in Queens and driven onto the island to be displayed in a six-foot deli case and then reheated in one of a battery of microwaves. There are two stools to sit on in this alleyway of a pit stop, but one typically eats along a narrow ledge running the length of the place, facing the wall, reading PSAs about the dangers of kohl, or various outward-facing missives from the Sikh community explaining how Sikhs, even though they have beards and wear turbans (actually *dastaars!*), aren't Muslim extremists.

I don't want to get bogged down by all the excellent details, like that the samosa with chickpeas and everything (a ladle of yogurt, a drizzle of sweet tamarind sauce, a dusting of *amchoor*-y spice mix, a shower of raw onions) is the "restaurant" dish I have eaten more times than any other, or how it's impossible to spend more than $8 per person there. Punjabi is important to me because it is open all day and all night, it is vegetarian, it is good, and it is in the middle of a very busy downtown nightlife neighborhood. It is a lifeline, a portal to another culture, a place for people from all walks of life—cab drivers and vegan goth girls and old-line Bolsheviks who moved to the

neighborhood long before it was douche-banker housing central—to rub elbows for barely any scratch.

New York is stocked tip to top with spots like that, though they take different forms. The canyons of midtown are speckled with twenty-four-hour bodegas—or "Korean delis," depending on where in New York you live and what they call businesses of that nature there. Inside, there are griddles manned by men in paper hats who will fashion you a hangover-slaying bacon-egg-and-cheese sandwich in less time than should be humanly possible.

Those sandwiches were a $3 splurge that was so worth it when I first moved to New York and was working as a receptionist who often needed something to take the edge off the night before. My best memories are experiences of texture more than flavor: crinkly, crumpled, shiny foil keeping a sandwich swaddled in steam-softened white paper piping hot; the kaiser roll crumbly, the fine corn-meal from its underside adding a pleasant grit to the assemblage; the bacon on the border of unbearably crisp but not too far gone; the egg, if eaten while magma-hot, still passably tender; squeezed-out packages of ketchup providing cool, sweet counterpoint.

Koreatown never fully goes to sleep, and in Chinatown, there's only a blink of the eye between when Great N.Y. Noodle-town pushes out the last group of drunk cooks who've spent a hundred dollars on Tsingtaos and heaps of Singapore *chow fun* and when the bakeries favored by tea-sipping grannies come to life.

Of course, when one starts getting into conversations about "ethnic" food, that's when the real Turkish oil wrestling kicks in, with food nerds reaching deep into each other's *kispets* to go for the kill. But there is nothing to talk about in an SF-versus-NY matchup unless "San Francisco" includes everything within a two-hour drive of the city center (which,

at certain times of day, is barely enough time to get over to the East Bay). Yes, there is more Mexican food there. But go and get shuttled through the line with brusque efficiency at Chelsea Market's Los Tacos No. 1 and you will end up with what are currently the best tacos in New York—where the tortillas have that fresh-masa magic, where the meat is charred by cooks who mean business, where, even though you are smack-dab in the middle of a yuppie food mall, there is no impeaching the quality of food you are unceremoniously served on paper plates, and which you would be happy to be served in East LA.

Perhaps it is more generous to take a shark-fighting stance here and give up my left arm (in the form of Mexican food) and bash the nose of the beast with a right-handed haymaker of Thai cuisine. It's not just that the Thai food is better here, which it is. It's that in the fifteen years that I've been paying attention, our Thai food scene has blossomed and matured. This kind of change is made possible by New York's size—because for whatever neighborhood is now hip and out of reach, there's always a new place to go—by new waves of immigrants bringing their food with them and new waves of eaters eager to try them. I remember being twenty-two or twenty-three when Mitchell Davis, a mentor of mine, took me to SriPraPhai, even then a destination, though it was in a space the size of a shoe box. Fast-forward a decade and a half, and SriPraPhai has expanded twice into neighboring spaces: it is now a landmark, an institution, with a tony, tiled fountain in its backyard patio—and it still serves the best very crispy watercress salad anywhere.

In that time, a dozen or more smaller Thai restaurants have opened around Elmhurst, slinging blindingly spicy dishes, serving up grilled cuttlefish and blood soup and raw shrimp and showing us that herbs like dill play in Thailand, too. When Andy Ricker docked his Pok Pok ship down on the Columbia Waterfront, it added to the dialogue, creating a regular stop where you could get a fix of *rau răm* or sawtooth herb. And after the closure of the last of the shitty spaceship-themed Thai restaurants that dominated Manhattan with sticky-sweet noodles in the middle-aughts, a new crop has started to flower—places serving what is putatively Isaan food, and which is often very good—especially when someone will bring it to you to eat in front of a movie at home.

And while I would stake the entire reputation of New York's eating scene on the shoulders of everyday places, something must be said for the establishments with the starched linens and sommeliers, for the places helmed by the chefs who reach for the stars.

I think it is worthwhile, perhaps, to tiptoe back in time. Delmonico's is too far back, maybe, and dwelling on the ripple effect of New York's steakhouse culture is too obvious. But modern restaurants are defined, in part, by the legacy of Joe Baum, who reinvented restaurants—or created a new concept for what a higher-end restaurant could be—in New York in the 1960s. With the Four Seasons and its ilk, he took restaurants from being eateries that rewarded the caste of their patrons with the appropriate-level service and made them into showy productions, places of democratic theater in the public sphere, cultural phenomena. This is a change that came to restaurants here, on the stage that only New York can provide, and then took over the world.

And where did the cooks who toiled under the chefs who institutionalized the French gastronomic dominance of the mid-twentieth century go to open their restaurants and make their names? New York. Chefs still whisper bedtime stories to each other about Lutèce and Soltner. (And they can still brush shoulders with him at a cooking school here.) Jacques Pépin washed up on these shores, directly from cooking for three French presidents. Jean-Louis Palladin suffered out of the spotlight in D.C. and came to New York too late for his genius to get its proper due, a penalty meted out on any number of chefs who have not made conquering New York part of their story. The city rejected Thomas Keller's restaurant Rakel—which, by all accounts, was exceptional and forward thinking and should have been beloved—and he retreated to the West to gather power before putting his stamp on the Time Warner Center. He opened in New York not because it made sense, but because owning a piece of the firmament here is one way to look yourself in the mirror in the morning and confidently say, "I am one of the world's greatest chefs."

But this is not an argument about history; it is one about eating. And the high-end eating in New York is challenged only by Tokyo in its diversity and quality. There is no one with a respectable breath in their lungs around to challenge that assertion. And to my comrade Mr. Chang's claim that fancy eating in Tokyo is better than it is here (put forth on page 64), I say this: there you get a facsimile, the best version someone can create of something somewhere else. Here, restaurants must bend (or they will be bent) to the city, their customers, their whims—they become of this place.

Alain Ducasse, God Himself among haute French chefs at the time, could not walk into town and dictate how we would dine when he opened Alain Ducasse at the Essex House. (I don't know that we were right to reproach him so, but in New York, New Yorkness often trumps what's right.) Look instead to how Daniel Boulud (first at Le Cirque), Jean-Georges Vongerichten (at Lafayette and then JoJo), and Mario Batali (at Pó) learned to navigate the desires of New York's café society, its bankers, its celebrities, its dumb kids out to celebrate an anniversary or a birthday, and how they turned those lessons into the models of modern luxury restaurants: Daniel, Jean-Georges, Babbo. These are places that are still somewhere between good and great to eat at, and that are imitated the world round, sometimes at franchises owned by their founders. This is to say nothing of the establishments (great and small) that have come and gone over time; we have lost more great restaurants here in the last decade than your city has opened in the last century.

And meanwhile the younger guard pushes ahead in the fancy-restaurant realm. Rich Torrisi and Mario Carbone's ever-growing colossus does not seem to stumble, bob, or weave even as it charges into deeper and more fraught waters. They have reimagined (without overly reconfiguring) Italian-American luxury at Carbone; they have opened an expensive-as-hell bagel shop that instantly won over a city of people who are very bitchy and opinionated about their boiled dough-rings.

Eleven Madison Park's Will Guidara, who trained under Danny Meyer (the man who turned a restaurant empire, an interest in Midwestern-style fast food, and a fetish for hospitality into a nine-figure IPO) and whose father held a high-up job for Joe Baum's restaurant company, helped resuscitate formal service and high-end front-of-house practices practically lost to time. A friend of a friend ate there and was surprised by an off-the-menu mid-meal course of nachos. It turns out Guidara's back office had stalked his Instagram, seen the evidence of nacho fever, and made arrangements. When you get past the craziness of what technology has made possible (thanks/you terrify me, geeks of SF), that is the very definition of white-glove bespoke service: the new version of a maître d' knowing the style of champagne you like to start your meal with, and having it ready before you even remember to ask. Except, you know, with nachos. Which are awesome.

Phew. That was a long list of white guys with fancy places that I'd need richer friends or better professional prospects in order to frequent. Let's have a drink, shall we? Because when it comes to liquid refreshment, you have come to the right city.

My preferred drink at most hours of the day is coffee. In the couple decades since I've been paying NYC taxes on my paychecks, the city's coffee culture has transformed. It was something I wrote about back when I used to get to print words in the *New York Times,* and it was Gregory Dicum, a San Francisco–based writer, who hipped me to the topic. I promptly dedicated myself to learning what was what in the cup.

Today, I have a very catholic view of coffee consumption: drink what you like. Whole swaths of my city get down with Café Bustelo and Illy, and, regardless of what I think about the beverage, my heart does somersaults like a baby golden retriever whenever I see somebody do the old-school deli-coffee shake: take it to the curb, invert the coffee in its flat-topped paper cup (preferably with that Greek-esque WE ARE HAPPY TO SERVE YOU design treatment), and shake it to make sure the gross quantities of sugar and milk that have been added to it are properly distributed. I'm a snobby coffee guy, to my financial disadvantage, and if you wanna go toe-to-toe on roasteries and quality cafés, I won't hear anything less than "we're peers." And I'd argue it's probably actually easier to get a cup of overthought bean juice in New York, there being fancy coffee places almost everywhere these days. Four Barrel is mighty, and I bow to its lumberjack swagger and size, but Abraço has more personality per square inch than anywhere, and its iced coffee is perfect, and Box Kite does a job that only Matt Buchanan could have a problem with.

Gosh. Things are a little tense here, aren't they? Maybe we should have a real drink to end this on a positive note.

Wine? Sure! I like grape juice as much as the next toddler, but drinking the stuff made by somebody who lives in a faux-château McMansion northeast of your city—somebody who's crammed a shitload of overripe fruit into an underaged barrel and fermented the results to port-wine strength—doesn't leave a lot of options for the rest of our night together. The tannins will rape and pillage our tongues, and the alcohol will keep us from a nightcap.

Maybe you've heard of Europe? See, in New York, we have a fantastic and wide-ranging selection of wines from that continent, imported carefully, wines at every point in the price and alcohol spectrums, wines fermented naturally and gently and expertly. Let's saunter down to Astor Wines & Spirits or Chambers Street Wines and pick up a bottle. Or we could go out to a wine bar—there's the Four Horsemen, hip as can be and stocked with great natural wines—and most restaurants have unpronounceable iterations of chenin blanc by the glass these days.

We could get a cocktail, of course, but I'm biased in that category, what with my brother being the guy behind PDT, one of New York's finer cocktail emporiums. That said, I don't mind if we duck into this anonymous bar here on the corner, a place that nobody's ever written about or is ever going to write about, and order a bourbon on the rocks.

See, one of the greatest things about drinking in New York is that, let's say we get carried away in there, and we end up sodden comrades, commiserating over the shared territory between our two cities—how money changes them, how all the old-line bars have closed or are getting taken over, how it's hard to afford anything anymore, how things are different than they were when we were first adults in our respective towns. The great thing is, we can do that until four in the morning, and assuming we don't go to eat something at that point, which we could do, we just stick our hands out toward the high moon or the brightening sky, and a yellow car comes and takes us wherever we're laying our heads.

Tomorrow we'll meet up for breakfast—have you ever had the sturgeon and eggs at Barney Greengrass on the Upper West Side? God, it's good!—and I'll let loose on the million and one things I hate about this godforsaken shithole. Because if there's one thing that New Yorkers are better at than eating, it's complaining about New York. I've really had to rein myself in. But that'll have to wait until the morning.

SAN FRANCISCO IS A DREAM

By Chris Ying

My choice to move to the Bay Area had nothing to do with food. I was eighteen and headed to college.

At the end of high school, my decision had come down to NYU or Berkeley. I chose Cal, partly because I liked that it had been a rallying point for the civil rights movement, and partly because my best friend and the girl I was chasing were both going there. Frankly, I had little idea where Berkeley was, except that it was obviously in Northern California, because I lived in Southern California and had never been. I knew even less about New York. I didn't know shit about shit.

Food meant *something* to me, but what exactly, I wasn't quite sure. I knew I liked eating more than other people did. At Berkeley, after spending freshman year in the dorms, most of us lived in groups of three or four or five in big, beat-up houses within walking distance of campus. But the farther away from campus you looked, the nicer the place you could land. Four of us moved into one floor of a bright, airy Queen Anne on Martin Luther King Jr. Way. It's less affordable these days, but in 2001, we had our own rooms, a spacious kitchen, a private yard, and parking spaces for seven hundred bucks a month each. My roommates and I shopped for produce at Berkeley Bowl, and I cooked often. I performed my first bit of woodworking in the front yard: an overly complicated but pretty picnic table where I could host dinner parties.

I gradually became aware of where I was. Berkeley wasn't a campus of disaffected intellectuals anymore; truth be told, it was mostly Asian engineering students. But there were still pockets of the local culture that remained true to reputation. The East Bay was still the home of Chez Panisse, Bay Wolf, the Cheese Board Collective, Acme Bread, Peet's Coffee & Tea. Berkeley Bowl was a grocery store unlike any I'd ever seen. It was minimally designed—concrete floors, exposed ventilation, laminated neon-paper signs—but I could lose myself for hours in the variety and quality of produce and bulk ingredients. The borders blurred between crunchy hippie fare and "ethnic" ingredients, EBT shoppers and well-off professors. I never really knew how much I liked shopping for groceries until I moved to the Bay Area.

I started watching a lot of Food Network. The inaugural meal on the picnic table consisted of homemade pizza (Mario Batali's recipe), macadamia-nut-crusted halibut with asparagus and coconut sticky rice (Ming Tsai's), and mango salsa (Bobby Flay's). I burnt a few macadamia nuts and dropped an entire glass platter of asparagus salad, plus the mangoes were too ripe, but the dinner was a hit among my easily impressed friends. I started cooking for them as often as I could. I tried replicating the Chinese food that I'd eaten growing up, and was surprised by how much people liked my home-cooked meals, amateurish as they were. I steamed whole bass in the microwave (still a pretty good technique!), and topped it with herbs, soy sauce, and smoking hot oil as I'd seen my parents do countless times. A frequent go-to was my uncle's ginger-scallion noodles: long threads of green onion, minced young ginger, and spaghetti-ish noodles with a thin wash of hoisin sauce. Weeknights meant stir-fries: onions stir-fried with flank steak, chicken stir-fried with asparagus. Like my dad, I added MSG to everything, in the form of a brand of seasoning called Accent.

Food—what to eat, where to get it—consumed a fairly large amount of my headspace, and I'm certain it would have been the same in New York. But I'm also fairly certain that I would never have become a cook or a cookbook writer or the editor of a food magazine if I'd moved to New York. Had I lived in New York, I imagine my aspirations would have culminated in visits to the restaurants of my TV heroes. In San Francisco, my wide-eyed goal was to cook like them. Sophomore year, I walked into a relatively new restaurant near campus and asked if I could speak with the chef about a job. The place was called Downtown. In spite of its patently terrible name—a reference to the restaurant's proximity to the Downtown Berkeley BART station—it was a good restaurant that occasionally flirted with greatness.

The chef, David Stevenson, had no reason to hire me. But he was a Cal alum himself, and quirky (a true softie in spite of a prickly outward bearing, I later learned). He looked at me with a skeptical frown from above his wire-rim glasses and beckoned me toward the kitchen. With a nasally voice, he asked the lead line cook, Kit, "Do we need any more people who don't know anything?" I could tell he was enjoying the discomfort he was causing.

"No?" Kit replied. I assume she didn't realize that I was the know-nothing he was referring to. For whatever reason, David hired me anyway.

I was a college student—soft, green, unskilled, untrained, a waste of space. But Downtown was an ideal learning kitchen. There was a raw bar, where I shucked my first thousand or so oysters; a brick oven, in which we roasted butterflied chickens and whole branzino; a grill station, where I learned to cook pork chops and New York steaks to temp; sauté 1 and sauté 2 for risottos, fish, and shellfish; and pastry in the back. I started on pantry, where my first attempt at frying fritto misto was laughable—the coating on the shrimp fell away like eczema, the calamari clumped into a mass, the fish was jerky. The sous chef, Jon, dumped it all out and walked me step by step through the process again. In three years, I rotated through every station. I made the best Caesar salad on earth (IMHO), fried untold numbers of olives stuffed with anchovies, scraped granitas, expedited service, learned how to taste wine (and drink Fernet), burned and sliced my arms (and once accidentally dropped a bandage onto a salad), fooled around with waitresses, and designed the posters for the live jazz performances on the weekends.

Would I have followed the same trajectory in New York? Would I have lived in a big house with a nice kitchen? Would a New York chef have let an enthusiastic novice walk in and start frying seafood? What I know now leads me to believe not, but that's beside the point. In Berkeley, while I was growing into a passable line cook, I was having the same transformative revelations about ingredients, cooking, simplicity, and seasonality that Alice Waters, Jeremiah Tower, and Judy Rodgers had three decades earlier. I was walking the same trails in the same woods. Downtown's owners and managers had come from the Chez Panisse family, and the school of cooking I was enrolled in was the olive oil–soaked, Mediterranean-inspired temple to farmers that Waters had founded a few blocks north.

On the weekends, I would wander around the farmers' market on Center Street in Berkeley, then later at the Ferry Plaza Farmers Market, when it reopened on the San Francisco waterfront in 2003. At Center Street, I could buy the same produce we were cooking with at the restaurant. At the Ferry Building, I saw cardoons for the first time and discovered the drippy sweetness of Frog Hollow peaches. My friends and I began to eat our way through Patricia

Unterman's *San Francisco Food Lover's Guide*, and despite that book's unrealistically optimistic portrayal of Bay Area dining, we had some memorable meals: burritos at Pancho Villa Taqueria, sugary mojitos and s'mores at Luna Park.

Don't bother tracking down either place anymore. Pancho Villa doesn't clock in among the seven best burritos in San Francisco, and Luna Park is sadly defunct. Unterman's affirmative outlook synced with the never-snarky, always-positive mantra espoused at the offices of McSweeney's and the *Believer* magazine, where I started working after college. It's an outlook that frustrates the hell out of New Yorkers, who are wary of everything all the time. When New Yorkers visit San Francisco, they tend to demand superlative dining recommendations—no doubt so they can measure them with their own finely calibrated judgments—and I struggle to provide them. I get excited about places like the House of Prime Rib, because it's an undeniably enjoyable dining experience, but I can see New Yorkers wondering if it's really the best or the first or the most special prime rib place.

New York has better food than San Francisco. I concede. I can be a painfully belligerent person, but I've never liked arguing this point. It's not that I don't love San Francisco or eating here. It's that I want this city to thrive, and the times we go wrong are when we start paying too much attention to the outside

world: when we try to make bagels or pastrami or barbecue or Chicago-style hot dogs. San Francisco is at its miraculous best when we are oblivious, blind to everything but the products and possibilities in front of us.

Diners are savvier in New York. It's true. I visited the city for the first time during my junior year of college. I loved dinner at Babbo and Otto, and second dinners at Gray's Papaya and the Halal Guys. After a few more trips, I caught myself looking at San Francisco with disappointment. San Francisco is one-tenth the size of New York, with an outsized reputation that creates unmanageable expectations. (Why else would we even be comparing them now?) It can be a dirty, unloving place. Our main food critic is myopic and antiquarian in his taste. It's easy to get discouraged about San Franciscans' historical lack of appreciation for talented fine-dining chefs. Daniel Humm worked here before opening Eleven Madison Park in New York. We had Laurent Gras at the Fifth Floor. For a while, Jeremy Fox was making the best food in the country an hour north, in Napa. Daniel Patterson recently left his position as head chef of Coi after nearly ten years of diligently trying to communicate his love for California to a stubborn audience. He found success, but I struggle to think of a harder-won victory.

But New York is also an echo chamber. It likes its own hype. (I'm sorry, but Great N.Y. Noodletown is gross. And how is an untoasted bagel better than a toasted one?) New Yorkers anoint heroes and stand by them—I should know, I work for one of them. If I spend a week in New York, it's possible (probable) that I'll go the whole time without speaking to anyone who isn't somehow involved with food. The eagerness with which New Yorkers praise their restaurants is enough to make you think that everyone in New York is eating well, but they're not. People eat terrible food everywhere. The foodies are just noisier out there.

Naiveté is what makes SF irritating as hell (see: the lines of people all over

town waiting for mediocre brunch), but it's also the key to its greatness. In 2004, I graduated from Cal and started cooking at Foreign Cinema, a concept restaurant that opened during the first dot-com boom and somehow managed to survive the bust. I worked for about a week on a grill the size of a half sheet pan before they cut me loose. I was coming into work in the afternoons, harried and tired after my morning internship at McSweeney's. I was slow and confused, and nobody was going to take me under their wing like they had at Downtown. On the bright side, I got to know Anthony Myint, another Foreign Cinema cook whom I'd met before but never really spent any significant time with.

In 2008, Anthony and his wife, Karen, started Mission Street Food: a weekly pop-up restaurant housed inside a Salvadoran *antojitos* truck. If New York is an echo chamber, San Francisco is a vacuum. People move to New York to be plugged into the pulsebeat of the world. San Franciscans, ironically, tend to be unplugged. None of us knew whether another cook had ever thought to sublet a roach coach and make his or her own version of street food. Anthony's idea felt completely novel and authentic. By the time Roy Choi rolled his first Kogi Korean-taco truck onto the streets of Los Angeles, Mission Street Food was moving into a new home in a dowdy Chinese-American restaurant down the street.

That sort of blind pursuit of an idea is evident in the best San Francisco creations. Mission Street Food evolved into its celebrated successor, Mission Chinese Food, when one of the chefs, Danny Bowien, decided on a lark to attempt cooking Chinese food. Tartine Bakery makes the best bread in the country and has influenced baking around the world, largely thanks to the quiet study and practice of its owners, Chad Robertson and Liz Prueitt. Saison, now a three-Michelin-starred restaurant, began as a pop-up on the patio of a café. The chef, Joshua Skenes, placed

a value on what he was doing and didn't allow the setting to change it. Peet's started the second wave of coffee roasting from a small storefront in Berkeley. Chez Panisse picked a fight with the food industry that we're still engaged in. Of course innovation happens in New York as well, but it's hard enough to be whatever you're trying to be without the crushing yoke of also having to be *New York* enough for New Yorkers.

I worry sometimes that San Francisco is losing some of its kamikaze verve. Like everyone else, I wonder if the tech corridor south of the city is changing, gentrifying, diluting the city's culture and driving up rent prices. The second coming of tech to San Francisco has so far yielded second-tier restaurant creativity: oversized sushi rolls and grilled cheese sandwich shops. I'm not sure whether to take heart in or umbrage at the San Francisco origins of services like UberEats and Caviar. I lean on them and I see everyone else using them, too. But are they representative of the sort of innovation we should come to expect from Bay Area food? I hope not.

Other questions persist. Why don't we have better Japanese food? Why are good vegetarian restaurants such a rarity, here of all places? Why is supermarket bread so terrible in the Bay Area? How can great Chinese food be so hard to find in San Francisco? Can this city really support any more Italian restaurants? I ask out of love.

New York and San Francisco have this in common: when you eat at the restaurants in either city, you know where you are. At Del Posto, Keens, Sammy's Roumanian, Barney Greengrass, you can't be anywhere but New York. The allure of visiting those restaurants is how close they make you feel to the city. The same can be said for the counter at Swan Oyster Depot, Dolores Park (with sandwiches from Bi-Rite or Tartine), a taqueria in the Mission at night, or a window seat at Zuni Café. The difference—and this could just be me—is how much closer you feel to the food here. 🆂🅵

PRODUCE

By Jonathan Kauffman

It's eye-rollingly redundant at this point to argue that the produce is better in San Francisco than in New York, at least ten months out of the year. Long before the city's Ferry Plaza Farmers Market became a tourist destination and Whole Foods brought organic dinosaur kale and *shishito* peppers to the masses, your average San Franciscan shopped for dinner at the Alemany Farmers' Market—both the city and state's oldest and arguably best farmers' market—or the Salvadoran and Mexican produce markets in the Mission, or the Chinese produce markets in Chinatown and the Richmond, or any of the Palestinian, Greek, and Vietnamese produce markets peppering our route home. Our kitchens are stocked with the Central Valley's excess.

A few months ago, I was interviewing Matthew Lightner at the Napa Farmers' Market. Last year, Lightner turned his back on the two Michelin stars he'd earned in Manhattan and decamped to Napa. One of his reasons, he said, was that Northern California's long growing seasons fascinated him. In New York, he'd get amazing tomatoes from the Hudson Valley, but two weeks later, their time had come and gone. California didn't become the nation's grocery basket because the soils here were any richer, or because, as we're all aware, the state had an infinite supply of water. California supplies the country with nearly half of its produce because we can grow fruits and vegetables all year.

Lightner's comment also shored up this theory I have that the reason the food is so good in San Francisco isn't just because the ingredients are so good. The food is so good because, from the late nineties to the late aughts, San Francisco was such a boring place to eat.

There was a moment—I'm going to ballpark it at 1996—when every mid-priced restaurant in town, or at least the ones that got attention from the press, decided that it would serve the same food as every single one of its competitors. "Farm to table" was everywhere, encouraging the fantasy that San Francisco was located somewhere between Nice and Genoa. Dining out was all heirloom tomatoes, chicories with fresh citrus, gremolata everywhere, and fritto fucking misto. Every restaurant had a beet-and-walnut salad. And because the seasons were so drawn out, you'd be eating that beet salad for seven months of the year.

I stopped getting excited about high-end restaurants during those years, which was problematic, because I was, for much of that time, a restaurant critic. It was hard to find anything new to write about or cooks who were doing anything new.

Things, however, were quietly heading in the right direction.

Chefs were so devout in venerating the perfect carrot, so desperate to clear out of nature's way, that they schooled themselves on how to properly cook vegetables: when to pull a roasted beet out of the oven so it would have the texture of a ripe mango; how to blanch and sauté green beans so that they were barely tender and still sweet. By the late 2000s, when San Francisco chefs finally decided to peek outside the cave, they had a granular understanding of when to buy persimmons or Tokyo turnips from their produce guys and how to slice, steam, roast, braise, dress, and season them.

Reinterpreting the scripture of California cuisine, touched but not enthralled by the avant-garde impulses of the mid-aughts, the best chefs in the Bay Area are now cooking with the flavors and textures of local produce in ways that are equally intuitive and oblique.

At Ninebark, Lightner's

Napa restaurant, the *hori-atiki* salad looks as if the chef has sacked a fairy camp and made away with all its microgreen jewels and flower crowns. At Al's Place, you wouldn't consider leaving without tasting Aaron London's sunchoke curry, its buttery sweetness set off by a profusion of citrus and sharp-fragrant greens. The best dish on Bar Tartine's fifteen-course New Year's Eve menu brought together a wobbly, ghost-white coin of beef tendon, sweet potatoes with papery-crisp edges, and the almost feral bitterness of broccoli rabe.

The fixation on the vegetable itself, not just what it can bring to a piece of meat, also gave rise to the market for ultra-specialty produce. Farmers began seeking out new heirloom varieties just to catch chefs' interests: Jimmy Nardello peppers, little gem lettuces, *spigarello* (whatever that is). Any variety that clicks with cooks shows up on menus all over the city, and the excess is sold to the public at higher-end farmers' markets. Those heaps of dinosaur kale and clamshell cases of Padrón peppers only arrived at Whole Foods because they were test-marketed, years or decades before, in San Francisco restaurants. **SF**

TKO: SF

A CLEAN, WELL-LIGHTED OYSTER BAR

By Rowan Jacobsen

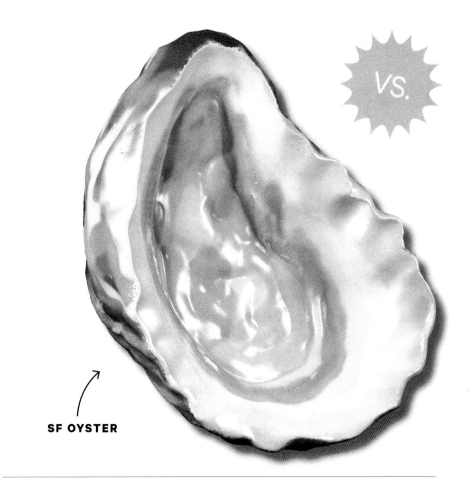

SF OYSTER

VS.

We were shucking oysters at the picnic tables at Hog Island Oyster Farm on Tomales Bay. The sun was low across the water, and a web of light danced on our glasses.

"Is it like this in New York?" she asked.

"No," I said. "You don't do this in New York." I handed her a Hog Island Sweetwater, and she tilted it into her mouth, then drank her wine. It was a rosé from a man in Sebastopol, in Sonoma County, and it was cold and sharp and tasted faintly of strawberries.

"Why not?" she said. "Why would you eat oysters any other way?"

The light was very fine and the hills shone like tawny elk, and the men from Hog Island were carrying bags of oysters from the boats up to the wet storage. "This is a good way," I agreed.

I shucked another dozen oysters with a knife that was attached by a cord to the picnic table, and we split them. The shadow from the hills across the bay had not quite reached us, and the ice under the oysters was melting and they were getting a little warm, but that too was okay, because we were outside.

"In New York they eat their oysters underground," I said.

She shuddered a little and looked out at the water. "How could they?"

"Grand Central Terminal," I said. "You eat the oysters at the oyster bar near the tracks as the trains come and go, and you sit at the old stools under the vaulted tile ceilings and drink martinis and it's very loud. And then you catch your train."

"And you like that?"

"Yes, because it's a stillness within the busyness. Every oyster is a moment of stillness. And you enjoy the stillness and the knowledge that you are about to be busy."

"That might be all right," she said.

I opened the rest of the oysters and ordered another two dozen and some ice. "It's more than all right," I said. "Even before Grand Central, all the oyster cellars in New York were in basements. You'd see a candlelit red balloon on the street and follow the steps down, and there would be sawdust on the floor. In New York, oyster eating still feels illicit."

She was watching the gulls fight over shells on the flats and thinking about the illicit people in New York eating their subterranean oysters. "I'd miss all this," she said. "To me, the oysters and the place are one." She was right. Even in San Francisco, the oyster bars are all glass and air. They are without fear.

"In New York, the oysters and the place are not one," I said. "The oysters should be from as far away as possible." I opened the oyster and cut the muscle very carefully with my knife, so I could see its heart beating coldly against its shell, and I tipped it into my mouth and popped its belly. "New York is all boxes of escape."

"Then why do you like it?" she asked.

"Because they are such good boxes. In New York, I can eat oysters from Maine, Mexico, New Zealand. Chincoteague. Nootka Sound. California. Here, it's all local." I shucked another oyster and handed it to her, and she stared at it for a while before swallowing.

"New York has no local oyster?"

"There is the Bluepoint. But it's dredged from Long Island Sound, so it's not that local, and you don't want to think about it too much."

VS.

NY OYSTER

"Does it taste like these oysters?" she asked.

"No. The Atlantic oyster tastes like wet rock. The Pacific oyster tastes like cucumber and kelp. It's from Japan. It always tastes a little bit like Japan."

"It's not native?"

"No, it was brought here after we wiped out the little native oyster. That one is very hard to find now."

"What does it taste like?"

"A little like licorice."

"Everything tastes like licorice," she said, "especially all the things you've waited so long for, like absinthe."

"That's the way with everything," I said. "But perhaps you haven't had the right absinthes." She didn't say anything. I shucked some more oysters and called for another dozen.

"Please stop shucking," she said.

"Nonsense," I said. "We've just started." I held another Hog Island Sweetwater in my hand. The shell was black and purple, and it had flared eaves, like a pagoda. I thought about how the Bluepoint's shell is thick and dull and built for the weather, like Cape Cod houses. "At Maison Premiere," I said, "in New York, they have an absinthe fountain. And their absinthes from Switzerland taste like forest herbs. And when you drink them with bitter Belon oysters from Maine, you lose the empty feeling and begin to be happy and to make plans. That is something you can never do in California."

"Because you never have the empty feeling."

"Because you never have the empty feeling." The water in the bay churned, and I thought about the San Andreas Fault a few feet directly below. I shucked another dozen oysters, set them on the tray beside her, and drizzled some cilantro-jalapeño-lime mignonette over the top.

"I wonder what they put on their oysters in New York," she said.

"Nada," I said.

"How dreadful."

"They used to use cocktail sauce," I said, "but now it's all *nada y pues nada*."

"California has lots of good sauces," she said.

"California has youth, and money, and sauces," I said. "California has everything."

"Perhaps you should move here," she said. "They all move here eventually. Even Mark Bittman."

She put an oyster in her mouth and swallowed very slowly. Everybody in California eats their oysters as if they had all day. In New York, you eat your oysters fast, reaching for them as if they were knots on a lifeline, reeling yourself toward whatever is at the end of a lifetime of oyster eating.

"There's something you need to understand," I said. "In the Northeast, the oysters are at their best on the winter solstice. It gets dark at five o'clock. A New York oyster bar needs to be well lighted, so the ice sparkles beneath the oysters. It needs to make good martinis. It must be clean and orderly. And it must stay open late, in case there is someone who needs it. I am of those who like to stay late at the oyster bar."

I shucked another oyster and handed it to her. She set it down on the tray. "Would you do something for me now?" she asked.

"Anything."

"Would you please please please please please please please stop shucking?"

We didn't say anything for a while.

"I am of those who like to leave the oyster bar early," she said at last. "So we can do sunset asanas on the beach at Point Reyes." The gulls suddenly erupted into the air. "Because time is an illusion, and I don't do scarcity thinking. There will always be more sunsets, and more oysters, and this place will always be here waiting for us, and whenever we come we'll have such a damned good time."

The water was sloshing in the bay. I watched our oysters quivering in their shells. "Yes," I said. "Isn't it pretty to think so?" NYC SF

COOKIE VS. COOKIE

New York City's
BLACK-AND-WHITE COOKIE

By Joanna Sciarrino

There's no question that there are better cookies in New York City than the black-and-white cookie. In fact, if I had to choose a favorite, it'd be City Bakery's melted chocolate chip cookie. No, the black-and-white cookie isn't New York's best cookie, but it is its most iconic—and it's not even a cookie.

It is a mostly dry, flat cake, covered in a sickeningly sweet cross between frosting and fondant in not one, but *two* flavors. Where else can you find such a confection? Fortune cookies are a dime a dozen (okay, $13 for a hundred on Amazon), and they come with every order of Chinese-food delivery for *free*. No one *intentionally* eats one: you just open it for the shitty fortune inside and end up involuntarily putting pieces of it in your mouth. It doesn't taste bad, but it certainly doesn't taste good. And when was the last time the fortune was actually worth it? Or made any sense?

A fresh and well-made black-and-white cookie, like one from William Greenberg Desserts or Glaser's Bake Shop on the Upper East Side, will run you about $3, which is appropriately expensive for a cookie of decent quality. They're not hard or dry or cloying—they're actually kind of delicious. So what if it doesn't teach you how to say "pants" in Mandarin? (It's *ku zi,* 裤子; now you don't even need the fortune cookie.) It's the size of your face and is both chocolate *and* vanilla. Like I said, it's not my favorite cookie on earth, but biting into a black-and-white immediately conjures visions of this fine, filthy city. Does the fortune cookie do the same for San Francisco? I didn't think so. 🔆

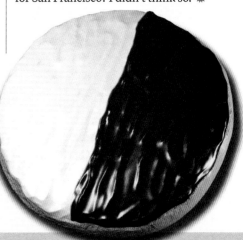

San Francisco's
FORTUNE COOKIE

By Rachel Khong

Every year, three billion fortune cookies are eaten worldwide. Numbers aren't even available for the black-and-white cookie, because nobody cares!

Jerry Seinfeld may have looked to the black-and-white cookie as an example of how we should approach racial harmony, but there's nothing so melting-pot as the fortune cookie. Fortune cookies tell a true American story. From San Francisco (where they most likely arrived by way of Japan in the early twentieth century), this not-Chinese cookie crept into Chinese restaurants and then American hearts. Black-and-white cookies, on the other hand, aren't particularly widespread outside of New York, and thank goodness.

Fortune cookies also have a touch of humanity to them. Until Edward Louie, owner of the Lotus Fortune Cookie Company in San Francisco, invented the fortune-cookie folding machine in the 1960s, the cookies were folded by hand and/or with chopsticks. (Cookies are still hand-folded at the Golden Gate Fortune Cookie Company in San Francisco.) And it's humans who thoughtfully construct the fortune inside your cookie. The fortune might be an astute observation: WHEN YOU SQUEEZE AN ORANGE, ORANGE JUICE COMES OUT—BECAUSE THAT'S WHAT'S INSIDE. Or a deep question, like: HOW MUCH DEEPER WOULD THE OCEAN BE WITHOUT SPONGES? A fortune might also suggest some lucky numbers for you. In 2005, a hundred and ten people played the same fortune-cookie numbers (22, 28, 32, 33, 39, and 40) in their local lottery and won! (Some of those fortunes read: DON'T BE HASTY, PROSPERITY WILL KNOCK ON YOUR DOOR SOON.) When has a black-and-white cookie ever won a person money? The answer is never.

Fortune cookies come in a much cooler shape. They're not too sweet, with a satisfying crunch. A black-and-white cookie cannot even be rightly called a cookie, because it's a cake: in a cookie-versus-cookie battle, it not only loses, it doesn't even qualify. ⚫SF

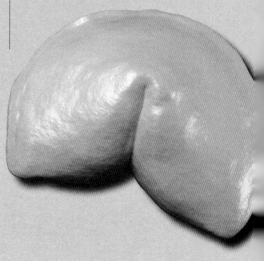

WINE COUNTRY

In a battle of the bottles, San Francisco Bay Area wines pummel those made in the state of New York. Nonetheless we put the question to two wine geniuses, Christina Turley and Erin Sullivan. Both worked as sommeliers in New York City before relocating to California. Turley is the director of sales and marketing at her family's winery, Turley Wine Cellars. Sullivan lives in St. Helena, in Napa County. She runs a retail company called ACME Fine Wines, and has a wine brand called Di Costanzo. —Rachel Khong

REGION VS REGION

ERIN SULLIVAN: Would the North Fork and the Finger Lakes be wine regions that we talked about if they weren't so close to the media hub of the universe, New York City? Maybe.

CHRISTINA TURLEY: The wine they can make in those two regions is pretty limited. It's a lot colder there and a lot more humid. Both of those factors are not super conducive to making a variety of wines. The Finger Lakes produces mostly aromatic whites: gewürztraminer, riesling, sparklers. Maybe cabernet franc, too.

ES: On the North Fork, for sure a little bit of cabernet franc, a little bit of merlot. Hardier grapes because it's so humid and cold.

CT: Whereas in California and the Bay Area—not just Napa, but Sonoma, Lodi, Contra Costa, Monterey, Santa Cruz, all of these places that are within an hour-and-a-half drive of the city—there's a huge range of soil types, of climates, of fog, all these other factors. I don't know that there's any argument about things like cabernet sauvignon, cabernet franc, merlot, chardonnay, sauvignon blanc—there's no way that any of the ones made in New

York are better than the ones made in California. California is the land of crops, and this is just another crop.

ES: I don't know many people from the Napa Valley who go to vacation in New York to go wine tasting. You might be able to taste a bunch of imported natural wines at an event or a restaurant, and that stuff is much harder to get in California because it just doesn't travel that well.

CT: I would say New York's proximity to beautiful imports from Europe at a better price is maybe one *slight* point that they get. You learn a lot about wine in a city like New York. But unless you travel, you get absolutely zero sense of what a vineyard is like, what a year is like, or anything about production. I have to say that part was the most fascinating thing about moving back and working at a winery every day: you could just walk around in the vineyard all day and actually see, okay, this is what this vintage is like.

ES: Now I think of our friends, my husband—people who make wine—and how many years of effort go into each bottle. I wouldn't have been exposed to that in New York. In St. Helena, we have proximity to these people and we tell their stories.

OLD AND NEW

ES: California has decades and decades of wine-making history.

CT: Exactly. Our oldest vines go back to 1885. And we have volume: California produces 90 percent of the wine made in the U.S.

ES: In California, too, we have a number of schools where people are able to study wine making. UC Davis, Cal Poly San Luis Obispo, and Fresno State are three that come to mind right away.

CT: And you can work in a lot of different places. If you want to learn to make pinot noir, you can drive forty-five minutes to Sonoma and make pinot noir. If you also want to learn to make cabernet, you can pop back over the hill and do that. You can be a winemaker who makes both, because they're that close by.

ES: And the barrier to entry for starting a new project in Napa Valley is actually a little lower than most people might imagine. We have friends who are maybe the assistant winemaker at a winery, and part of the terms of their employment is that they get to make a few barrels of their own project on the side. There is room for innovation, and there's room for smaller projects in Napa, which I think keeps it an exciting place.

CT: I think there is a sense of awe and wonder in what we have and what is possible here, and also a constant state of experimentation. In the Old World, in Europe, they have laws in every wine region, and you are not allowed to put this region on your label if you're not making the two prescribed grapes that are allowed in that region. Whereas in California, we can basically do almost whatever we want, and people are constantly redefining themselves. We're the place of old vines and young love. **SF**

PIZZA

From: Peter Meehan
To: Adam Kuban

Hey Adam,

The next issue of Lucky Peach is the "Versus" issue. Our big feature is a New York vs. SF package.

I know there's great pizza in SF—they have Una Pizza Napoletana, and in the greater Bay Area, the Chez Panisse–style pizza obviously was influential. But NY pizza is the best, right? Or the biggest? Your work on pizza during the heyday of Slice was the finest pizza writing ever committed to the page, and having your take on this would make me very happy. Whaddyasay?

Best, pfm

From: Adam Kuban
To: Peter Meehan

I'm not sure I'm feeling pizza-y enough to write this, if that makes sense. I have been trying to summon some spleen and find I have very little spleen left to vent on pizza or pizza rivalries.

Yes, of course, NYC TKOs SF on this. I LOVE San Francisco, and there are some wonderful pizza joints there, but it can't hold a candle to NYC's pizza culture.

I say *pizza culture* here, because I'm reading two different things into your question. Maybe I'm taking liberties… On the face of it, you say, "NY pizza is the best, right?" But to make this apples-to-apples, we would necessarily have to assert that there is an "SF-style pizza," and there isn't. There are many, many fine San Francisco *pizzerias*—a bunch of which have sprung up in the last decade, and some of those

are making pizza that haunts my greasy pizza dreams, pizza that is world-class and maybe even at the very pinnacle of whatever genre it is an exemplar of. But IMO they are all still making versions of another locale's style.

So in my mind, I have rejiggered this exercise to NY pizza culture vs. SF pizza culture. And… NY still TKOs SF.

To me, I don't even think you can be called a pizza city unless you have an indigenous style of pizza. NYC actually has an indigenous style of pizza. You might even make an argument that we have *three* or more indigenous styles.

There's the classic NY slice pizza, the kind you find on almost every block and which most of the country and/or world takes to be "New York pizza." This is the thin, crisp-yet-foldable slice that drips grease down your wrist as you scarf it while walking down the street. It's the most common style in the city, the kind of pizza blanketed with low-moisture (i.e., *not fresh*) mozzarella and a slightly sweet, acidic sauce. And there's also its predecessor, the "New York–Neapolitan," which is what traditional old-world Neapolitan pizza morphed into here in the city's old coal-oven bakeries. There's sort of a pizza continuum, going from the true Neapolitan stuff—small individual-size pizzas, cooked in a wood-fired oven, topped with crushed San Marzano tomatoes and fresh *mozzarella di bufala* or *fior di latte*. Southern Italian immigrants, who landed in NYC, began baking breads with coal ovens (because coal is easier to ship into the city), which they then used to make pizza. The pizzas became bigger and crisper than back in Italy. Cow's milk mozzarella becomes the standard for lack of water buffalo in the

U.S. Eventually low-moisture mozzarella becomes the standard, as do smaller gas-fired pizza ovens, and the slice shop starts to proliferate, leading to the New York–style pizza we know.

Then you have what we call "Sicilian" pizza here in New York—the thick-crusted pan pizzas that locals also call "square pies." They're based on the traditional Sicilian *sfincione*, which are decidedly more minimal—similar crust, but topped with a thick paste of chopped onion, tomato, and anchovies and dusted with a hard cheese, like *caciocavallo*, and bread-crumbs. NYC's Sicilian pizza is a take on that, but reinvented. Sure, you could argue that New York–Neapolitan and Sicilian as we know them are just bastardized versions of Italian stuff, but hey, we've been doing them long enough and there's a critical mass of pizzerias making them, so we have time and volume on our side.

But there is no "SF-style pizza"—certainly none that could be ID'd easily by Jane Q. Pizzaeater—and even if you generously open it up to "California-style" pizza, that's more about the toppings than an overall set of traits or pizza-genre gestalt.

That said, there seems to be the seed of something that may eventually become an easily recognizable SF style, and you've covered it in *Lucky Peach* before—the Chad Robertson/Tartine crust, which you see influencing PizzaHacker and even the folks at Mission Chinese Food in NYC. It's a naturally leavened dough with a high hydration, which simply means it's got a lot of water in it, which in turn leads to some glorious hole structure, most evident in the crust at the edges. Throw some inspired, fresh Cali toppings on there—heck, look at the Early Girl dry-farmed tomatoes a lot of places are turning to—and that may coalesce into a style.

Call me in fifty more years and we'll talk.

—Adam
adamkuban.com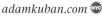

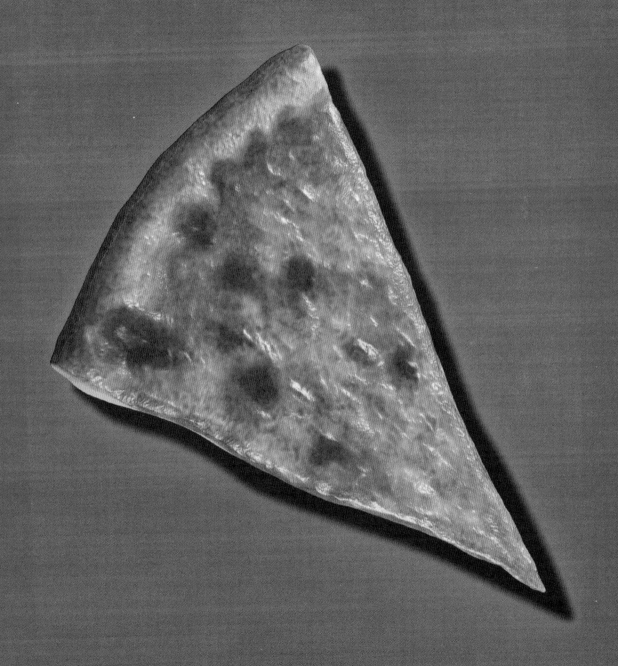

BURRITOS

Words and photographs by Walter Green

San Francisco is the best city in the world for burritos. Or maybe it's not—I can't be sure. If you're reading this as a Los Angeleesi or a San Diegonian and getting upset, calm down, it's just my opinion and I'm just one person. But also, *can't you just let us have this one thing? Do you really need to be so greedy?* When someone comes to visit me here, I can either take them to a taqueria or a park where someone tries to sell you weed cookies every minute. What else am I supposed to show them? The Twitter building? Just let us have good burritos, please.

What I'm arguing for here today is the Mission burrito, named for the neighborhood it originated in: the Mission. Both Taqueria La Cumbre and El Faro claim to be the OG. La Cumbre, who say they sold their first Mission-style burrito when they were still a meat market, in 1969, has recently even gone so far as to repaint its exterior bright red with tall white letters proclaiming it THE BIRTHPLACE OF THE MISSION STYLE BURRITO, whereas El Faro stakes their claim in the form of a small sign that says they've been selling this style since 1961. So I guess La Cumbre wins, based on the size of their sign.

THE INGREDIENTS

It varies a bit from place to place, but for the most part what you'll get when you order one (aka a "super burrito") is a flour tortilla, filled with the meat of your choosing, rice,[1] beans, cheese, sour cream, guacamole (or just avocado), and salsa. All wrapped in foil.

You might think this sounds like a lot, and it is (especially compared to the more pared-down burritos of East LA), but that's kind of the point.

THE PRICE AND THE SIZE

For some, it's too much. The tortilla is pushed to its absolute limit. When it comes time to roll a Mission burrito into a taut cylinder, it must be wrapped *with* the foil, or else the filling will all come spilling out. This is a hefty, inexpensive meal (around $7–$9) whose sustenance you can spread out over the course of a couple days (if you're reasonable), or eat in one five-minute session (if you're me or someone like me).

THE FOIL AND THE MOBILITY

As an idiot, I think it's just a fun tactile experience to unwrap your first bite, like a mini Christmas for your mouth. Make sure you unwrap as you go, not all at once. Again, the foil is essential to the structural integrity. If you want to walk around as you chomp down on this thing (though I'm not sure why you would, are you really that busy?), the foil will keep your burrito intact as you move. If you decide halfway through that you've had enough, you can just fold your excess foil over the top until you're ready to take on the leftovers.

**SHEER VOLUME AND
THE QUEST FOR THE BEST**

Ask ten different San Franciscans what the "best" burrito place is and you're likely to hear ten different places, for ten different reasons. Some of the reasons might include: *Oooh, they griddle the tortillas here longer*; or *Wow, the proportions of each ingredient here are *just* *perfect**; or *This place is close to my apartment.* The truth in my experience is, at most taquerias,[2] specifics like this change burrito-to-burrito, depending on the day of the week and who's at the griddle.

Beyond the certified greats—El Farolito, Cancún, La Taqueria, which are all within six blocks of one another!—what makes San Francisco a burrito paradise for me is the fact that you can walk into almost any taqueria with a small amount of money and leave with a reliable burrito. Even if we don't have the best burritos, at least we've got the most good ones. **sf**

---

1 LIFE HACK: One of the main complaints you'll hear about a San Francisco burrito is, Oh there's so much rice! They cover up whatever good flavors are actually in there with all! that! rice! Are you a human who's eaten in restaurants before? Just order it without rice, it's fine, you'll be fine, everything will be fine.

2 They're called "taquerias," but most people order burritos, not tacos. Maybe because the tacos in the Mission are mostly just small open-faced burritos. Or maybe because "burriteria" sounds funny.

SANDWICHES

By Robert Sietsema

Though the name for this bread-and-meat assemblage is—according to legend—attributed to England's fourth Earl of Sandwich, it was perfected and diversified here.

Indeed, restaurants specializing in sandwiches first appeared in New York around 1924, evolving from lunch counters that would move upwards of seven hundred sandwiches per day. Look no further than Gotham for the origin of the Italian hero, the breakfast sandwich on a kaiser roll, and, perhaps most iconic of all, the pastrami sandwich.

Some say that New York pastrami originated in Romania, but that's absolute hogwash. The pastrami eaten there, called *pastrama,* is a Turkish import—a leathery beef product dry-cured with salt, red pepper, and fenugreek, sliced thin like prosciutto, and dry as a desert wind. Our pastrami, invented around 1900, is a moist brisket that has been brined and cured with black pepper, coriander, and garlic, among other spices, then smoked. It is steamed to juicy perfection before it is served piping hot on rye bread.

At Katz's Delicatessen, where superior pastrami is found, the deli man pulls a whole blackened brisket from the steam cabinet, plops it down on his cutting board as proudly as a dog presenting its owner with a just-caught bird, then cuts it with a sharp knife into thick, fatty, pink slices (the pastrami, not the dog). These he deposits on slices of rye that is delivered to Katz's in wax paper–wrapped loaves of distinguished New Jersey origin.

As he makes your sandwich, the deli guy cuts a couple of especially good slices of pastrami, lays them on a saucer, and slides it across the high glass counter, allowing you to sample the flavor of the meat as you watch the assembler put the knife under the inches-high stack of sliced brisket and scoot it onto the bottom piece of rye. Then he slathers the top piece of bread with grainy mustard of Eastern European heritage before crowning your sandwich with it. Before handing it to you, he cuts the sandwich in half along the middle, and puts a good handful of brine-pickled cukes and green tomatoes on the plate.

And what does the pastrami sandwich look and taste like? The meat has been stacked in such a way that it's thicker in the middle than at the edges. Liberals take a giant sloppy bite out of the middle; conservatives nibble judiciously around the edges, saving the greater wad of meat till last. Both take bites of pickle between bites of sandwich to clear the palate and enhance the saltiness of the already-salty meat. All the while, there is a cacophony going on around you in the tumultuous dining room of Katz's as customers nosh and kibitz, plates and silverware rattle,

canned soft drinks *fffzizzappp* as they're opened, people drop things, and steam rises from the pastrami, corned beef, and plain brisket like a deliciously edible vision of a Russian steam room.

Of course, the towering cultural achievement that is the pastrami on rye is just one of a half-dozen unimpeachable examples of archetypal sandwich excellence that the city calls its own. The name *gyro* was first applied here to the Greek pocket sandwich, sometime around 1970. And the meatball hero has been exported around the world in the New York raiment it was first dressed in: long loaf, melted skullcap of mozzarella, tomato sauce oozing at the edges. New York is the adopted home of the Cubano, with its irrational combination of meats and cheese melted in the warm embrace of the sandwich press with margarine and mustard and two pickle slices.

In Brooklyn, one finds the *vastedda*—a small roll smeared with ricotta and melted *caciocavallo* and layered with crumbly sautéed cow spleen. In every nameless deli across the city one can score a breakfast sandwich on a kaiser roll with egg, American or cheddar cheese, and a meat of your choice (as long as your choice is bacon, boiled ham, or sage-scented breakfast sausage).

And look to nearby Saratoga Springs— where New Yorkers used to go every

summer to watch the ponies race in the salubrious air of the sub-Adirondacks—to find the 1894 (contentious) origin of the club sandwich. The club on toasted bread, cut in quarters and heaped to surreal heights with chicken, bacon, and roughage, came back down on the train and took its rightful place in the pantheon of New York sandwiches without peer.

Under the onslaught of anti-carb mania, the sandwich has suffered in many parts of the country, where bread has been replaced by lettuce in twee little wraps. Not so in New York. Not only has the sandwich culture survived, but new sandwiches are being feverishly created every day. Some are invented by indigenous sandwich concerns, others by sandwich interlopers that have flocked here from other places to luxuriate in the sandwich-friendliness of New York.

Recently, Bunk Sandwiches sailed in from Portland, Oregon, bringing with it a vegetarian sandwich of marinated chickpeas and feta, and a new twist on the tuna melt made with fish from the Pacific Northwest. Meanwhile, British sandwich chain Pret A Manger has blanketed the city with new branches. Old-fashioned delis have fought back with newly coined sandwiches featuring ungainly combinations of ingredients, spinning off every kind of wrap, burrito, and panini they can think of.

Hipster pizza parlors and butcher shops have generated their own sandwich culture, the former basing their sandwiches on the venerable Italian hero, the latter on heretofore unexplored meat combinations and treatments. The Brooklyn butcher Meat Hook now has a shop serving a pig-face sandwich and another sandwich with roast pork slathered in tuna mayo; somewhat perversely, their vegetarian sandwiches are often the best of all. Not to be outdone, Boomwich, descended from a pizza parlor, offers a cheesesteak in which the cheese has been partly replaced with crumbled Flamin' Hot Cheetos. Crunch, crunch.

Indeed, in New York, the sandwiches only get stranger and better. But that's just part of living in the World's Greatest Sandwich City. What city can match us? None. 🏙️

VS. WORST FAMOUS DISH

San Francisco's
CHOWDER BREAD BOWL

By John Birdsall

If you're a tourist, you and the kids at the Wharf, zippered up against a morose and penetrating gray, you will probably come to know San Francisco sourdough as a thing with the heart pried out of it.

You might nibble at the plug, three inches thick and three across, cut from the top of a Boudin Bakery mini loaf that has been trepanned with surgical precision, the innards scraped out and flushed with chowder. This chowder, however, not the bread bowl, will command your attention. It is jiggly, a turgid suspension of fishy fatty acids: here a lump of potato, there an orange-hued clam stiff as a Chiclet stuck to a bus seat. You'll eat as much as you can with the thin compostable spoon and throw the bread away, or leave it for seagulls to raid with practiced claws. Why wouldn't you?

To be picked by scavengers is a tragic end for a loaf, but the true tragedy here is the tarnish the clam chowder bread bowl leaves on one of San Francisco's great food legacies. The clam chowder bread bowl is a disgrace, a criminal misuse of flour, water, salt, and microbes.

Other cities appreciate bread. They like a nicely turned out *boule,* a *bâtard* that's fat in the middle and tapers to sharp little elbows with nice chew, a shapely rye. In New York, like a lot of places, bread rustles in plastic bags of slices, brackets for pastrami or egg salad, essential but not *essential,* the way Tartine's country

loaf is. The sliced face of Tartine *levain* is human in the most intimate way. Put it to your cheek and it's clammy, like a child's hand; huff it and it emits the complicated sweet-sourness of something alive.

I grew up in a family where San Francisco sourdough was daily food. My dad expected it on the table every night, unless we were having tacos or the snow pea–beef stir-fry my mom made on the counter in her electric skillet. There were four in our family. It took us two days to eat a loaf of Larraburu Brothers—one of the big industrial sourdough brands that ruled San Francisco for decades before petering out in the 1970s. Even

our suburban Safeway south of the city got bread deliveries twice a day, the regular morning loaves and an afternoon supplement for people to pick up after work. You could identify the latter both by their warmth and by a Day-Glo sticker on the paper bag that told you: LATE BAKE.

Still, it was a time of decline in San Francisco bread. My mom remembers a small neighborhood bakery, Ruby Bakery, in San Francisco's Bayview neighborhood in the forties, where she would sometimes pick up the nightly loaf for her grandpa. "You had to get there by three, because they'd sell out and then just close. It was a

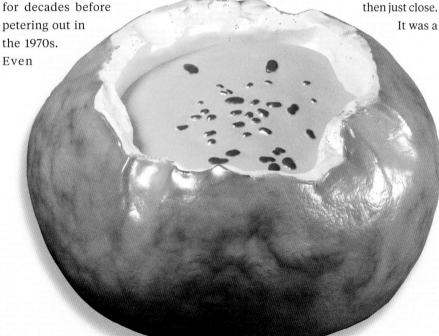

husband and a wife and a daughter—French from France," she says, "and the bread was wonderful."

Steven Sullivan, cofounder of the Acme Bread Company, became familiar with one of these smaller San Francisco bakeries in the 1970s, when he was a kid washing dishes and bussing tables at Chez Panisse. It was where the restaurant got its bread.

"There was still one of these bakers, Venetian Bakery, baking baguettes in a stone oven, probably, a coal or gas burner, and they made really good baguettes," Sullivan says. "I'd eat them spread with tons of butter and the vinaigrette left in the bowl from somebody's dinner salad, and it just seemed like one of those things that was perfect."

Venetian Bakery closed, and Chez Panisse moved on to new sources. But after a few months, Sullivan says, "the owner would opt for some more-automated process, and the bread would lose its character." Sullivan was baking bread at home,

as a hobby—a fact that didn't escape Alice Waters.

"Alice," Sullivan says, "in her special way of finding something that somebody is doing with passion and mapping that onto the mission of the restaurant, made me the bread baker."

It was a fractured line of tradition, since Sullivan was inspired not by the big San Francisco bakeries like Larraburu and Boudin, but by the ferociously elegant *pain de campagne* from Poilâne in Paris, and the scholarly 1977 Elizabeth David book, *English Bread and Yeast Cookery*. By the mid-1980s, Sullivan's Acme bread had completely remade the image of San Francisco sourdough as *pain au levain*.

About twenty years later, Chad Robertson, Liz Prueitt, and Tartine Bakery would bend the arc of San Francisco bread history again with their country loaf, simultaneously advancing and cementing the city's status among the bread capitals of the world. In San Francisco, we're into the ecosystem of grains and millers, of

starters suckled quietly over decades while the world goes loudly to hell, of scarred metal deck ovens and slowly moving lines stretching into the parking lot of Acme early on Saturday morning—twenty of us in hoodies waiting to buy a couple of spiky *pains épis*, a loaf of walnut levain, and a rye raisin roll to eat in the car.

As affronts go, the clam chowder bread bowl might be more ridiculous than offensive, the souvenir Alcatraz sweatshirt for tourists. After all, good bread has almost always coexisted here with the not-so-good, the handmade loaf you line up for, praying there's still one on the rack by the time it's your turn, and the mass-batched one you can get at the supermarket at two a.m. Maybe diversity is the ultimate mark of supremacy in this city of bread, where invisible yeasts swarm like plankton in the cool, restless air. **SF**

New York City's
DIRTY WATER HOT DOG

By Mark Bittman

We know memory is inaccurate, and this notion that we remember things better as they become distantly past is absolute bullshit. (It could be that I'm not old enough yet.) I do, however, remember walking to the Barnes & Noble flagship on 18th and 5th sometime in the late sixties to sell a pile of textbooks, at which point I went outside and proceeded to buy and eat seven Sabrett hot dogs (15 cents each) with mustard (spicy brown) and onions.

Could I possibly have eaten seven hot dogs, or is this simply some story I tell myself? More to the point, could I possibly have eaten seven hot dogs if they were as terrible as the New York street hot dogs

of today? (Which now cost $1 or $2; you almost never know until you ask or pay.) It's hard to believe.

I did not have the most sophisticated palate in the world in 1966. But I grew up a) near a kosher deli that griddled its dogs until crisp, and served them with *fiery* mustard on a not-too-soft, toasted roll, and b) near a Nedick's, whose decent dogs were served on a beautifully toasted roll, with babyshit-yellow mustard relish that had its endearing qualities. If there was one thing I could judge, it would seem it was street hot dogs.

Right now it is a race to the bottom between pizza-by-the-slice and the hot dog. (We'll save the pizza for another time, though it is interesting to note that the 99-cent variety, which has taken over, is not much worse than the $2.50 option.) The hot dog is a *shondah* for the *goyim*, which basi-

cally means it makes New Yorkers look bad. It's usually served just above room temperature, held warm all day long in tepid water (somehow not a breeding ground for bacteria). It's never crisp, which a hot dog must be to be good. It's served with bland mustard, bland sauerkraut, and/or a mix of what appears to be the sauce strained from SpaghettiOs and onions softened by, no doubt, irradiation; these, too, are bland.

There appears to be no way around this. Undoubtedly some weirdly fine "gourmet" dog will appear, and it'll be pretty good, and it'll cost $7, and the lines will be around the block; perhaps this has happened already. But it might be better if the New York dog would go the way of the Parisian dog-in-a-spiked-baguette that was once so popular, and disappear. Roasted sweet potatoes on every corner would be an upgrade. 🐾

The best coast is up for debate.
The best websites? No contest.

Build a beautiful website with Squarespace.
Start your free trial today.
www.squarespace.com

LA

CRÈME CARAMEL LA

TALESAI

BELLA JULIA

SADIE

FUNDAMENTAL

BARREL DOWN

MAISON GIRAUD

JOHNNIE'S

JOSS CUISINE

ORLEANS & YORK DELI

HAWKINS HOUSE OF BURGERS

GOLDEN ROAD

EDEN BURGER BAR

ALL'ACQUA

GOOD GIRL DINETTE

MY VEGAN

WOODCAT COFFEE BAR

PEZ CANTINA

LEDLOW

EGGSLUT

BĂCO MERCAT

EDIBOL

AZLA VEGAN

BIRRIERIA JALISCO

TNT TORTAS & TACOS

PANXA COCINA

NYC

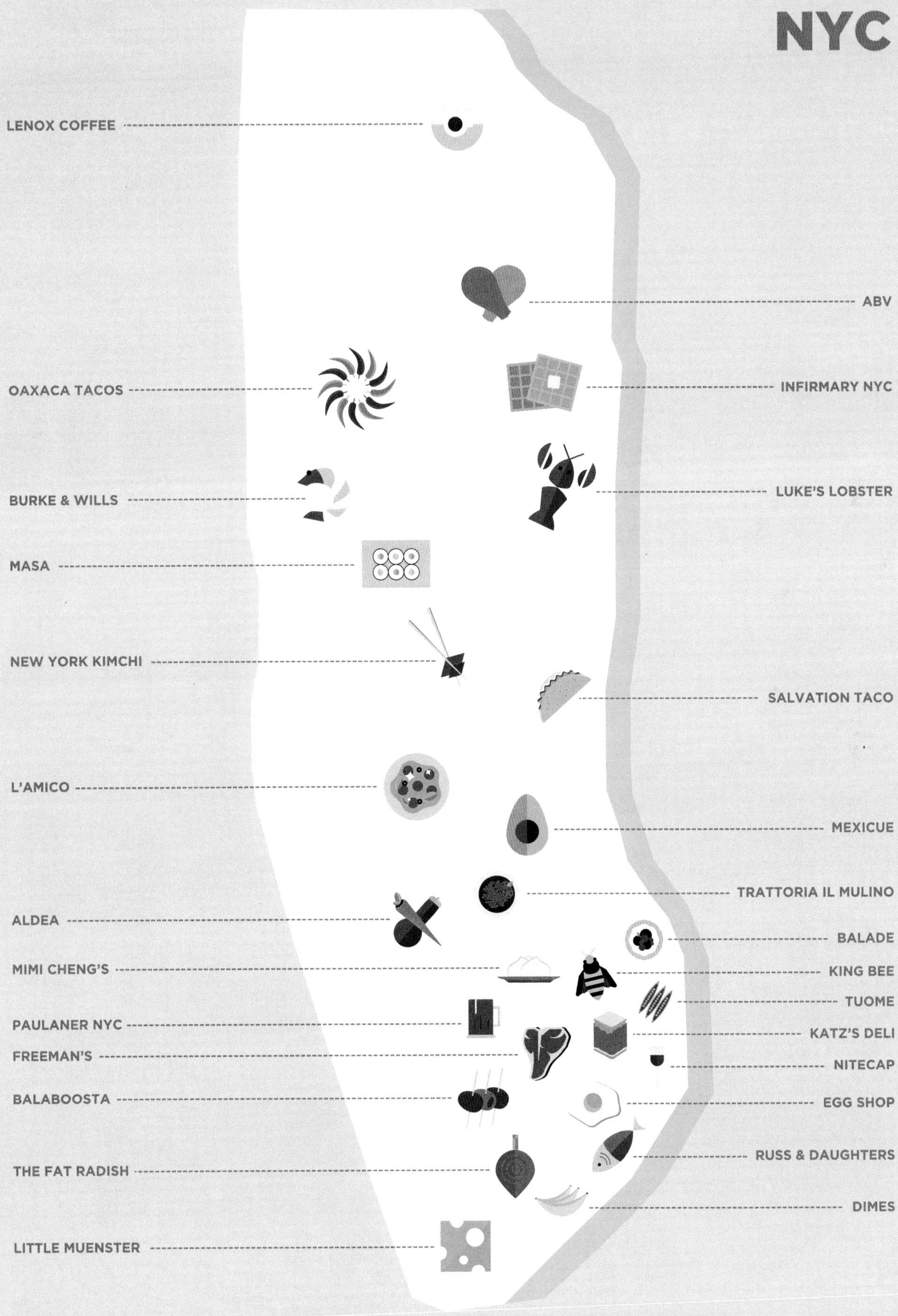

LENOX COFFEE

OAXACA TACOS

BURKE & WILLS

MASA

NEW YORK KIMCHI

L'AMICO

ALDEA

MIMI CHENG'S

PAULANER NYC

FREEMAN'S

BALABOOSTA

THE FAT RADISH

LITTLE MUENSTER

ABV

INFIRMARY NYC

LUKE'S LOBSTER

SALVATION TACO

MEXICUE

TRATTORIA IL MULINO

BALADE

KING BEE

TUOME

KATZ'S DELI

NITECAP

EGG SHOP

RUSS & DAUGHTERS

DIMES

Chicago's Madison Street runs east–west, beginning at the downtown tourist scrum that is Millennium Park, past the United Center where the Bulls and Blackhawks play, through Garfield Park and its magnificent conservatory, and in front of MacArthur's, the West Side soul-food restaurant that counts Barack Obama among its loyal customers. It ends a little more than eight miles from where it started downtown, at Austin Boulevard, where Chicago turns into the village of Oak Park.

There might not be a more culturally and psychically significant thoroughfare in town. It's not so much what's along the street, but what it divides: separate identities, separate allegiances, separate ways of life—practically speaking, two distinct and fiercely territorial versions of Chicago. North Side from South Side.

Most locals gravitate to one of these two Chicagos; you either identify as a North Sider or a South Sider. Yes, this is a generalization (there also exists West, Northwest, Southwest, and Southeast Side communities), but it's easiest for residents to grasp the narrative of us versus them. In very broad strokes, North Siders are affluent, Cubs fans, Wieners Circle patrons, O'Hare Airport users, Wilco band members. South Siders are working class,[1] White Sox fans, Jim's Original patrons, Midway Airport users, Chance the Rapper. Our food culture is likewise segregated. For example, nearly all the Michelin-starred restaurants in town lie north of Madison. Conversely, you'd be hard-pressed to find many aquarium smokers—the cooking vessel favored by black Chicago barbecue pitmasters—on the North Side.

If you're the kind to play favorites, the distinctness of these two versions of Chicago makes it easy to choose sides. I've never had to, or more accurately, I've stayed above the fray—there's much to appreciate with the food contributions from both sides of town. I would happily maintain my isolationist stance, but as that seems not to be enough for this magazine, let's look at this empirically.

1 Let me quantify "affluent" and "working class." The city delineates an official "North Side" district comprising five of seventy-seven community areas, and an official "South Side" with twelve. (There's also a "Far North Side," "Southwest Side," "West Side," etc.) The city also publishes quantifiable evidence that shows North Siders living better lives than their South Side counterparts. One data point the city uses is called the "hardship index," which uses six socioeconomic indicators to calculate a score for each community area (e.g., percentage of households living under the federal poverty level, percentage of persons aged twenty-five and over without a high school diploma). The community areas on the North Side averaged a score of 15.6 (out of 100) with an average per-capita income of $48,136. The South Side averaged a hardship score of 59.25 and an average per-capita income of $21,658.

NORTH SIDE

EXHIBIT A:
DEEP-DISH PIZZA

The great misconception about Chicagoans is that deep-dish pizza is the food of the everyman. The secret that Big Pizza doesn't want you to know is this: the overwhelming majority of deep-dish-pizza consumption within Chicago city limits is done by tourists.

Thumb to the wind, a good 90 percent of all deep-dish pizza in Chicago is served in the downtown neighborhood of River North, where it was purportedly invented in the 1940s, and where mainstays Pizzeria Uno, Lou Malnati's, and Gino's East have locations. It is, to put it mildly, an indulgent meal that requires pile-driving with fork and knife through thick layers of tomato sauce, cheese, sausage, and dough. It is essentially an Italian meat casserole baked in a hubcap. That said, deep-dish pizza will forever occupy our city guidebooks and be recommended by concierges, even though it's not representative of the pie most Chicagoans order: locals prefer the tavern-style pizza, its crust thin and cakey, the toppings predominantly sausage and cheese, and cut into square pieces instead of triangular wedges. Deep-dish pizza is undeniably a Chicago product—one that is best consumed in River North.

EXHIBIT B:
STEAKHOUSES

The steakhouse is synonymous with Chicago dining, yet there's little that sets a Chicago steakhouse apart from a steakhouse anywhere else. There's no iconic dish that gives it local distinction, save for perhaps the chicken Vesuvio—bone-in chicken and potatoes wedges sautéed with olive oil and white wine, a dish popularized in Chicago.

Chicago steakhouses became known for both their quantity and ostentatiousness. Steakhouses were the representative restaurant genre in the city in the last century. The high-end steakhouses of River North are storied (Gene & Georgetti, Gibsons, Morton's), but the discount lunchtime steak emporiums in the Loop were also popular, especially for businessmen before the advent of fast-food take-outs (steakhouses like Ronny's, or Tad's, where a full steak meal cost $1.09 in the sixties).

Today, all the best steakhouses are clustered within two miles north of Madison Street. (In a 2013 *Chicago* magazine feature on the city's best steakhouses, all top twenty were located on the North Side.) They will also cost you at least $100 a head, but for all their three-piece-suited decorum, bebop blasting, and maître d's looking for a twenty for preferred seating, at least the ribeyes are seared at 800 degrees, the spinach creamy, and the accompanying drinks stiff as Sinatra's goons.

EXHIBIT C:
HIGH GASTRONOMY

If you 1) once subscribed to *Gourmet,* or 2) are a wealthy European or Japanese businessman who travels the world with a *Michelin Guide* in a death grip, or 3) know who Michel Bras is, the Chicago food scene you love resides almost entirely on the North Side. In the last forty years, one could make the case that Chicago was home, on three separate occasions, to America's best restaurant.

In the seventies and eighties, wealthy out-of-town diners would fly into Chicago (technically in the northern suburb of Wheeling, but North Side in sensibilities) just to dine at Le Francais, home of Jean Banchet, Chicago's first celebrity chef. Then came Charlie Trotter in 1987, whose eponymous restaurant in the Lincoln Park neighborhood pivoted luxury dining from a cuisine rooted in French to one more idiosyncratically American. In 2005, that torch was passed again to a young chef named Grant Achatz, whose forward-thinking restaurant Alinea opened a couple blocks from Charlie Trotter's and has achieved three-Michelin-star status every year since 2011.

These last twenty years have seen Chicago become a creative wellspring of fine dining. Our city has bred Rick Bayless, Stephanie Izard, Paul Kahan—all of whose flagship restaurants reside north of Madison.

EXHIBIT D:
ETHNIC NEIGHBORHOODS

The names of certain North Side streets are signifiers for their ethnic restaurants. Tell friends you're dining on Devon Avenue and it means you're eating at a Hyderabadi, South Indian, or Pakistani restaurant. Argyle Street means you're eating Vietnamese. Along Milwaukee Avenue, north of Belmont, most likely you're having stuffed cabbage rolls and pierogi at a Polish restaurant.

Albany Park is the neighborhood equivalent of a Benetton ad: a mix of Mexican, Filipino, Korean, Middle Eastern, Serbian, and Croatian enclaves, and I'm probably missing a half dozen others. Humboldt Park, several miles west of the Kennedy Expressway, is where much of the city's Puerto Rican community resides, and is home to one of Chicago's lesser-known culinary exports: the *jibarito,* a steak (sometimes pork) sandwich with aioli and vegetable fixins, but with fried plantain chips in place of bread.

SOUTH SIDE

EXHIBIT A:
CHICAGO HOT DOG

Serving steamed wieners in snug lengthwise buns isn't a Chicago invention, but the specific construction known as "dragging through the garden" is our city's culinary gift to the world. Picture the Great Depression. Times were lean. To stretch an all-beef hot dog into a more satiating meal, vendors bulked up the sandwich with an assortment of vegetables and condiments. Eventually, those toppings were codified into a specific, unwavering combination: a pickle spear, tomato wedges, raw white onions, relish, sport peppers, mustard, and a dash of celery salt. You can trace these toppings to the Greek, Eastern European, German, Jewish, and Italian immigrant communities who built Chicago in the city's early days. This is a hot dog that embraces its sense of place.

Though the hot dog quickly became a citywide hit, its original center of gravity was in the Maxwell Street neighborhood on the South Side, where the Vienna Beef Company was originally headquartered. This area was the city's Jewish quarter during the turn of the last century, and it was Vienna Beef's owners who scored a hit at the 1893 World's Columbian Exposition with their kosher all-beef wieners.

EXHIBIT B:
ITALIAN BEEF

The Italian beef is another sandwich born from scarcity. It's not too far off from a french dip: beef cooked in Italian spices is shaved and served sopping wet in a roll, then topped with an oily bricolage of pickled vegetables called *giardiniera*. The most popular origin theories point to two entrepreneurs around the time of the Depression, named Pasquale Scala and Tony Ferreri. Both served food at weddings, shaving rounds of roast beef into paper-thin slices and serving it in its juices on a roll, so as to stretch out the meat. Soon, it became a bona fide business venture along Taylor Street in the South Side Little Italy neighborhood, but it wasn't until after World War II that this garlicky mess of a delicious beef sandwich found popularity in all corners of the city.

EXHIBIT D:
THE LESSER-KNOWNS

There are indigenous dishes that even most South Siders will never have tried. To wit, the mother-in-law sandwich, a tubular tamale served in a hot dog bun and smothered with chili. Or the Jim Shoe, a monster mash-up of roast beef, corned beef, and gyro, combined against the will of structural engineering into one sandwich. Then there's the Big Baby, prominent on the Southwest Side at Greek take-outs named Nicky's (many are unrelated businesses), that's essentially a flattop-seared double cheeseburger with the specific toppings of mustard, ketchup, pickles, and a tangle of grilled onions. There's nothing particularly unique about this burger assemblage, but slap a catchy name on it and Southwest Siders will embrace it with the fiercest of loyalties.

EXHIBIT C:
TIP-LINK COMBO

The 1920s saw a wave of African-American laborers, many from the Mississippi Delta, migrate north and resettle in the South Side. A number of them brought a penchant for cooking meats over live fire.

Eventually, South Side Chicago–style barbecue crystallized as a singular method of cooking. The key is a four-sided plexiglass pit known as an aquarium smoker. It has no dials, electronic settings, or automatic shutoffs. It's heated from below with wood fire, a garden hose delivers smoke and moisture, and the gut intuition of the pitmaster controls the grill. When it comes to South Side barbecue, the two principal cuts of meat are the rib tip—the knobby, fatty end of the sparerib—and hot-link pork sausage. Head to iconic take-outs, like Barbara Ann's or Lem's, and you'll hear every other customer utter the words, "Tip-link combo, please."

CLOSING ARGUMENTS

It all comes down to perspective. Present-day versus historical contributions. If you're a restaurateur with a modicum of ambition, most likely you're hunting for a space north of Madison Street. The North Side is the land of plenty, with its gastropubs and neighborhood Thai restaurants and bespoke gluten-free bakeries to keep your Instagram feed fed. It is where you go if you're an out-of-towner dining in Chicago.

On the other hand, almost without exception, Chicago's most interesting dishes, the ones with the longest staying power, were born from South Side neighborhoods, where life's a bit more hardscrabble. Limitations breed creativity—the Italian beef and Chicago hot dog being the poster children for this idea. In other words, while our deep-dish pizzas and celebrity restaurants are worthy ambassadors to the world, in terms of the side of town that best reflects the people, the time, the place, the city, it's gotta be the South Side. **LP**

TOKYO VS. THE WORLD

by David Chang

It's pointless to engage in any debate about which city has the best food without mentioning Tokyo.

Tokyo is the answer I give when friends and I kick around the question, *Where would you live for the rest of your life solely for the food?* Why? Because Japan as a country is devoted to food, and in Tokyo that fixation is exponentially multiplied. It's a city of places built on top of each other, a mass complex of restaurants.

Let me rattle off the reasons why Tokyo beats all other cities:

It has more Michelin stars than any other city in the world, should you choose to eat that kind of food. I'd argue that some of the best French food and some of the best Italian food is in Tokyo. All the great French chefs have outposts there. If I want to eat at L'Astrance, I can go to Tokyo and eat it with Japanese ingredients. The Japanese have been sending their best cooks to train in Europe for almost sixty years. If you look at the top kitchens around the world, there is at least one Japanese cook in nearly every one.

Japan has taken from everywhere, because that's what Japanese culture does: they take and they polish and shine and they make it better. The rest of the world's food cultures could disappear, and as long as Tokyo remains, everything will be okay. It's the GenBank for food. Everything that is good in the world is there.

If I want to have sushi, there's no better place on the planet. All of the best fish in the world is flown to Tokyo so the chefs there can have first pick of it—whether it's Hokkaido sea urchin or bluefin tuna caught off of Long Island, it all moves through Tsukiji fish market before jokers in any other city get a crack at it.

If I want to have *kaiseki*, there are top Kyoto guys who have spots in Tokyo, and they're pretty fucking good. If I want to visit places dedicated to singular food items, from tempura to *tonkatsu* to yakitori, they've got it all. They have street food, *yakisoba,* ramen. They have the best steakhouses in the world. They have the best fucking patisseries in the world. The best Pierre Hermé is in Tokyo, not in fucking Paris. You know why? Because of the fucking Japanese cooks. I can eat the best food in subways, I can eat the best food in the train station, I can eat the best food in the airport. It's the one place in the world where I have to seek out bad food. It's hard to find.

They have no stupid importation laws; they get the best shit. Europe exports their best shit to Japan, because they know the Japanese have better palates than dumb Americans. It's true. Go to the local department stores and buy cheese. It's amazing.

The produce is the best. It's the best in the world, in my opinion. I'd argue Japanese produce is the best because it's not the equivalent of a beautiful dumb blonde who just looks great. It looks great *and* it's got brains. From root vegetables on up, somehow they just grow the best shit.

The best chicken in the world, the best eggs in the world, the best beef in the world (if you like that kind of beef). Shit, the McDonald's there still cooks their french fries in beef fat. It's awesome.

I can craft a great meal from convenience stores. A fantastic meal. From properly made bento boxes, to a variety of instant ramen, to *onigiri,* to salads, to sandwiches, it's all really good. The egg-salad sandwiches at all the convenience stores are amazing. All the fried chicken, delicious. The chain restaurants, amazing. KFC, Pizza Hut, TGI Fridays, Tony Roma's, you name it. I've been to all of them. Guess what? They're all awesome. You know why? They care a little bit more. That's it. They just make better fucking food than anywhere else. It's awesome.

Now let's keep it interesting by switching and going over the cons. There really are only a few.

There's no real Southeast Asian food that I know of. But guess what, I'm not looking for it. If it exists, it's probably really good. That's what you need to understand: generally, everything in Tokyo is better than what you can have anywhere else.

They don't really have slices of pizza. But guess what New York doesn't really have much of anymore, either? Slices of pizza. Tokyo does have pizza, though. Their Italian food is great.

Tokyo doesn't really have Spanish food. But you know what I don't ever really eat? Spanish food. I don't have to eat paella ever again. Spain's a country I like to visit, but we're talking about foods that I generally eat or I want to eat on a day-to-day basis.

I genuinely don't give a fuck about any other place on the planet. I just want to go to Tokyo to eat. Look at the other food cities in the world, such as Paris. Can't live there, because I don't want to eat only French food. It's great for a week and then you know what I want? Anything but French food. Same thing with Italy and Italian food. I think it's got to be the most boring food culture in the world. For fuck's sake, can you eat anything besides fucking pasta?

You know what I eat in New York? Japanese food. And Japanese food that's based on what's in Tokyo. I save money to go to Masa. I don't understand why this is even a question in the Versus Issue. Everyone else should just bow down. Tokyo is like the Borg, because they take from everyone else and they make it better.

Everyone who argues for anyplace that isn't Tokyo is saying Salieri was a better composer than Mozart. No. Fucking. Way. It's like arguing that there was a better basketball team in 1992 than the Dream Team. It's not even worth anointing a second-place winner—it's ridiculous.

Maybe you're wondering, *If you like it so much, why don't you open a restaurant there?* I'm scared. It would be like being the best basketball player on a European team. I'd feel like Toni Kukoč getting on the court with Pippen and Jordan and being like, *Oh, this isn't fun. I suck.* That's my great fear. It's not like swimming with sharks. I'd probably be the shark coming to Tokyo. But little fish eat sharks in Tokyo. **LP**

The Miraculous Mr. Hai

Interview and photographs
by Calvin Godfrey

Dry shafts of sunlight pinged off glossy banana and durian leaves. A diesel-powered ferry waltzed over the chocolate-milk surface of the Mekong River. The island of Ngu Hiep breathed a dizzying floral perfume. I was looking for Thai Van Hai, 67, aka Hai Cut ("Hai the Cripple"). Every man, woman, and child I asked knew the way to his low brick home.

Hai grows durian and plays a dying genre of music once popular in the surrounding delta, where happy people set their lives to sad song.

For generations, farmers here have partied to ballads of loss, betrayal, and bereavement warbled over notes plucked from scooped-out fretboards. The music, known as *tai tu*, sounds like something Hank Williams would have played on an opium bender in the South Pacific.

During the Vietnam War, whole operas of these songs filled theaters throughout the south, and it's thought that wealthy patrons paid their favorite artists in gold bars. After the war, the genre atrophied into the stuff of blind beggars, hustlers, and buskers. Hai Cut plays these songs, against all odds, with just one hand.

How has Ngu Hiep changed since you were little?

The name means "five villages." Back in the day, each village was pretty sparsely populated, and there were no paved roads. Everyone lived in poverty. My father worked his own rice paddy and as a hired hand. My three siblings and I did our best to help out on our little farm. They hadn't built the dike yet, so our rice paddies flooded all the time.

I used to run around and shoot birds and catch fish. When I got older, I'd get my brothers and neighbors together over rice wine or tea to play the guitar and sing. That was the tradition back then. All my neighbors played, and I developed an interest in music pretty quickly.

Do you remember the day you lost your arm?

I was ten years old; I'd taken my family's water buffalo out to pasture. All of a sudden, gunfire exploded from across the river—I was in the middle of a battlefield! When the shots died down, a few of my neighbors ran over and helped me. The war affected us a lot. There were bullets and bombs all the time. We were just a poor family caught between both sides.

What were your days like afterward?

I stopped going to school. I'd never been much good at it anyway, and I'd lost my writing hand. So I kind of just helped out around the house. Because of my condition, I didn't have to work the fields until I was twenty-two, so I had lots of time for the guitar.

A master who was famous throughout the region lived just behind my house. He had a very simple life. He was broke. He worked in the fields and barely messed around. Nobody else wanted to teach a one-handed student; it was hard enough to teach a man with two hands. I told him not to worry about it—I knew I had it in me to learn. Some people dropped out early because they didn't have the talent. Others couldn't practice because they had to go to work. I guess they weren't destined to keep going. So I told him to ignore me and just let me watch and learn. He treated me just like everyone else, but he refused to take any money for teaching me.

When did you start to work as a musician?

For a while, music provided my main income. I couldn't do heavy labor so I'd use the money I made with music to hire neighbors and cousins to come help me plant, harvest, and work the farm. Word spread about the one-handed guy who played the take a boat. I began to travel all over the Mekong Delta and ended up in Soc Trang, where this music was really big. People there just took me in. I ended up teaching my future wife's brothers and sisters, and they decided to fix us up.

Did you fall in love straight away?

I didn't really want to settle down at the time. But I guess destiny pushed us together. She wasn't very beautiful and I wasn't very handsome. But she was good at taking care of things. We got our own little house and I taught music. We lived in Soc Trang for eight years before we packed it up and came back to the island.

Why did you come back?

I was about twenty-six. My parents decided to carve up the ancestral land and gave little parcels to my brothers and me. The war was really tense at that point. But I'd always wanted to come back. I was sorta homesick.

Did the war continue to affect your family?

Yeah, my parents were always saving up to build a little hut out of palm fronds. We'd get it up and live in it for a while. Then planes and helicopters would come by and blow the thing to shreds. Luckily, we were always out in the fields when they came. We'd pitch a little tent and stay in that until we could save enough to build it

again. It usually took about ten days to put together a shelter.

When did life around here start to get better?

When I was about forty, a few people started planting durian. Everybody slowly realized we could make more money and do less work by growing durian rather than rice. People began by planting the island's famous bitter-melon varietal* from seed and sharing cuttings from the best trees. They were delicious, but the flesh was too thin, the seeds too big. We've since grafted Thai varietals onto our old rootstock. Now most trees yield about one hundred dollars' worth of fruit every harvest. I have forty small trees that yield about a ton of durian a year. When I'm not playing music, I spray and water my trees. I pay friends and neighbors $7 a day to help do any work that requires real strength. I only make about $1,000 a year from durian.

Most months I play a couple weddings and funerals. But in the last five to seven years, the music game has gotten much harder. Back in the day, every wedding and funeral needed someone like me. Nowadays, it's one in ten. For all the rest, people just play junk pop or karaoke, which requires no skills whatsoever. When I do get a gig, I'm lucky if I walk away with $15 in tips. In a lucky month, I make $50 playing music and singing. I have three students who pay me $50 a month. But

whenever friends come over, I stop what I'm doing to play. There's always time for drinking and playing music.

How do you get to your gigs?

I strap my guitar to my back and drive. Earlier this year, I took a shortcut over this narrow concrete bridge I've crossed over a thousand times. Something went wrong with my brakes, and I dropped five meters into the muddy canal below.

Oh my God! Did you go to the hospital?

Nah, some neighbors heard the splash and fished me out. I was fine.

What about your guitar?

Yeah, fine too.

And your bike?

We just changed the oil and it was fine.

Man, why do you try so hard?

I dunno. When I recognize there's something I have no chance of succeeding at, I won't make the effort. But when I feel I've got something I have a slight chance at, I'll go after that thing.

Are you happy with your life?

To a certain degree. I feel like it's been a pretty complete and happy life. Of course, I have dreams. But you've got to know when to drop them. **LP**

---

*WHAT THE HECK IS BITTER MELON DURIAN?

Historians say that durian first arrived in the Mekong Delta in the holds of Chinese junks at the end of the nineteenth century, but locals believe a martial-arts master planted the first tree in Vietnam after returning from a romantic exile in a durian orchard somewhere in the Khmer Empire.

When neighbors turned up their noses at the fruit's infamous odor, the aged master promised a flavor "as potent as young love" before collapsing into a fatal coma. The fruit's Sino-Vietnamese handle sau rieng means "my sorrow." Hai Cut claims Ngu Hiep developed its orchards cautiously at first, planting seeds only from the tastiest trees. At some point, the bitter melon varietal (sau rieng kho qua xanh) emerged as the best loved.

"No one knows where it came from," said Dr. Nguyen Minh Chau, who ran the government's Southern Fruit Research Institute from 1994 until

2014. "It was widely established when we opened our office." Known by its thin husk, dark color, and large seeds, the bitter melon durian eventually fell out of favor as Vietnam edged into capitalism and consumers began clamoring for brighter, bigger, fleshier fruit.

Dr. Chau and his team held contests to identify more commercially viable varieties that farmers could graft onto old rootstock. One lucky farmer claimed a first place prize for the Ri6 durian, which Dr. Chau says outdid all contenders for sweetness, heft, and brilliance. The farmer, however, died the following day. Nevertheless, bitter melon trees fell by the score as farmers rushed to get in on the new fruit. While bitter melon durian remains renowned for its tastiness, nowadays, the fruit retails for a pitiful 30 cents a pound when you can even manage to find it.

69

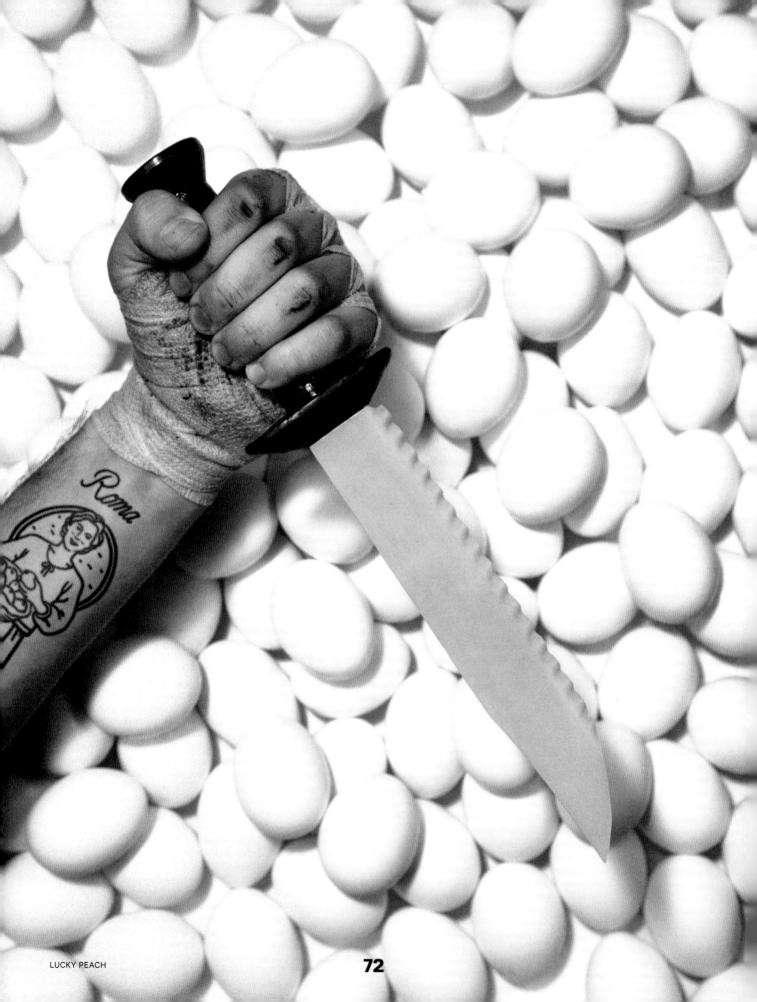

73

CRUDE OF

BY BRIDGET HUBER

THE GODS

PHOTOGRAPHS BY CHRIS VON AMELN

At the edge of a tide-drained mangrove swamp in Bahia, Brazil, Fabio Silva Santos is tending a sawed-off steel barrel as it steams over a smoky fire. He's cooking *dendê* fruit that he brought back yesterday from an island across the way. The fruit is shiny red-orange with a black tip. It grows in bunches on tall palm trees and has a stringy, weirdly greasy pulp around a seed that's like a little coconut. Santos, 37, is shirtless, dimpled, and wearing jean cutoffs that ride low. He's making palm oil the old-fashioned way.

Along the nearby roadside, stands sell bottles of rust-colored palm oil. Highway BA-001 passes Santos's house in the Maricoaba district of Valença, as it cuts through a lush, hilly landscape known as the Dendê Coast. It's called *azeite de dendê* here, and it lends Bahia's food its orange color and unique taste—one that's earthy, like turmeric, and reminiscent of a perfumy chicken broth. Dendê oil has been the lifeblood of Bahia's food culture and religious life for more than three hundred years.

Palm oil is the most consumed oil on the planet—and all of it starts out something like the oil Santos is making: dark orange and smelling of dirt and flowers. This is crude palm oil. By the time palm oil reaches most of its consumers, it will have been refined, deodorized, stripped of color, and rendered so neutral that it's hard to even perceive that you're eating it, or applying it to your face, or lathering your hair with it. But we all are—it's in about half of the packaged products sold in supermarkets worldwide: cookies, shampoo, lipstick, soap, instant noodles, doughnuts, toothpaste, packaged bread.

Though there have been reform efforts, the palm-oil industry has a terrible reputation of pushing orangutans toward extinction, destroying the jungle, contributing to global warming, and abetting junk food's march across the planet. Though dendê oil has long been a symbol of Afro-Brazilian identity and resistance, in recent years, the country has been pursuing a new frontier for palm oil in the Amazon region, one that its proponents hope will help Brazil get a piece of the huge and growing global market. I came to see both faces of palm oil in Brazil, the sacred and profane.

Once the fruit is cooked, Santos uses a metal shovel to transfer it in batches to a waist-high mortar that he carved from a hardwood trunk. The pestle is a long, heavy club. Dendê oil made like this, called *dendê de pilão*, isn't that common anymore, but it's prized. And pricey: it costs about twice as much as other oil. There are a few bigger factories in the region that make palm oil that's sold in supermarkets, and dozens of small, mechanized mills that supply mostly local markets. Santos used to work at the latter before starting to make his own oil. "My grandmother did it, and I'd seen other people do it," he says, mashing in a circular motion. "One day I said, 'I'm going to do it.'" He sells to locals and restaurants and says there's always demand.

After more than an hour, the fruit has become a fibrous paste full of large black seeds. It goes into a plastic basin that's the size and color of a kiddie pool, but deeper. While Santos is working, a small channel of water refills the mangrove and friends come and go in dugout canoes with outboard motors. Others come from the highway, bumping across the yard on motorbikes.

"*Vamos lá,*" Santos says. Let's go. It's time to "wash" the dendê. Santos pours warm water over the pulp, then he and I reach in up to our elbows, along with his mother, who everyone calls Carminha. We agitate the mash, and the liquid starts to separate—clear orange oil on top, muddy ocher wastewater below. Santos skims off the oil and dumps it into a pot to cook it one last time.

As Santos is working, his wife, Eliza, cleans flat, silver fish that come from the mangrove. Eliza has a sweet face and a white hairnet. She takes me to the house to make *moqueca,* a fish-and-dendê-oil stew, for lunch. The family runs a small bar, and Santos sleeps in a tiny room behind it. Eliza joins him when she's not working cleaning seafood on a touristy island nearby. The room has a narrow bed, a fridge, a stove, and a muted TV currently showing what looks like a bus race. Eliza puts a mortar and pestle—a small basalt one, about one-fiftieth the size of Santos's—on the dresser and grinds hot *malagueta* peppers, half a tomato, an onion, and cilantro together, along with a sour green fruit called *biri-biri,* but you can use lime instead. She puts a few big glugs of Santos's oil in a wide, shallow pan. (Eliza doesn't use coconut milk, but most people do and they add it at this point—about as much coconut milk as the oil.) She adds the paste from the mortar and then lays the fish in whole, covers the pan, and puts it over a low flame. Moqueca can be made with shellfish, eggs, or even chicken or soy, Carminha tells me, but good dendê oil is the essential ingredient, and handmade is the best. "What kills the moqueca is bad dendê," she says.

We borrow a plastic table from the bar and Eliza brings out big plates of moqueca, rice, and beans for Santos and me; she and Carminha decline to eat until we're done. "They're embarrassed," Santos says.

The stew is deep yellow-orange, and the oil's earthiness is cut by the sourness and spice and the fish's mild flesh. We drink cup after tiny cup of beer from liter bottles. If a bottle isn't icy-cold, Carminha says, "This beer is hot!" and sends someone to the bar's overburdened refrigerator for another. At some point a finch-sized green

parrot, a family pet, hops over to me. It perches on my finger and accepts bits of rice. When Santos and I go down to check on the oil, the mangrove is almost full. He'll let the oil simmer until the fire dies, then bottle it. He thinks he'll get five or six liters of oil, all of which are spoken for. Santos clangs the lid back on the pot and takes the final swig of his beer, then flings the cup over his shoulder into the water.

There are lots of different oil-producing palms, and some are native to Brazil, but the oil palm that has conquered the world is the African oil palm, *Elaeis guineensis*. As its Latin species name implies, it's native to the Gulf of Guinea region, which stretches from Ghana to Gabon, though humans have been helping the plant expand its range for thousands of years. The tree has long met all kinds of needs, both mundane and metaphysical. The Yoruba considered it sacred. The fronds were used to thatch roofs and make mats and baskets. The fruits were made into wine and vinegar, the oil used for cooking and to make soap. And it had

mystical qualities: the fruits were used to divine the future and the oil used in ceremonies. On the African continent, there are at least 332 different names for the oil palm.

Today, palm oil is the most widely traded and cheapest vegetable oil on the market. The oil palm is superefficient. It produces more oil per acre than any other oil-bearing crop—twice as much as olives and ten times more than soy, according to Brazilian government figures. Between 2000 and 2012, global palm-oil production more than doubled, and it's only expected to keep growing. In the U.S., we are consuming more palm oil than ever. That's partly because palm oil, which stays solid at room temperature, is a good substitute for partially hydrogenated oils. A federal ban on partially hydrogenated oils will take effect in 2018.

Most of the world's palm oil is produced in Malaysia and Indonesia, where plantations have devoured huge tracts of the rainforest that is home to critically endangered species like the Sumatran elephant and orangutan. Tropical rainforests sequester large amounts of carbon, which

is released into the air when they're cut. More recently, Indonesia's palm industry has started burning peat swamps to clear land, and it's been likewise disastrous for the climate. Around the time I was visiting Santos in Bahia, thousands of peat fires were burning in Indonesia. On many of those days, Indonesia was emitting more greenhouse gases than the U.S. Consumers and activists have exacted promises from some of the biggest palm oil companies to end deforestation in their supply chains, but it remains to be seen how they'll put the promises into practice.

The oil palm has been growing in Bahia since at least the eighteenth century. There's no definitive account of how that happened, but its arrival was tied to the transatlantic slave trade. An estimated 40 percent of all slaves taken from Africa—some four million people—ended up in modern-day Brazil, more than any other colony in the Americas. (For comparison, 500,000 slaves are thought to have been brought to North America, about 5 percent of the total.) Most of the slaves who ended up in Brazil were brought to work in the mills and sugarcane plantations that ringed the Bay of All Saints.

"The African oil palm and its products played complicated roles in slavery-based societies," writes Case Watkins, who spent two years studying palm oil in Bahia as a Fulbright scholar, and wrote his doctoral dissertation on the subject. It "offer[ed] familiar nutritional, spiritual, and medicinal nourishment to enslaved Afro-descendants while also helping to facilitate the brutal trade that possessed them." Slaves were fed dendê-enriched gruel during the Middle Passage and there is evidence that women made dendê oil on the ships, Watkins says. When the ships landed, slaves' bodies were rubbed with dendê oil to make them shine before being auctioned. Many slave traders also traded in dendê oil, and, after slavery was outlawed, used the oil trade as a front for continued human smuggling.

Some say dendê began growing here by happenstance: animals could have dug the seeds from the garbage and scattered them, or they could have been dumped from ships' hulls. Others believe the tree was planted on purpose. Locals say the trees were planted by vultures. However it got here, it's thrived in Bahia.

Today, there are some palm plantations in Bahia, but most dendê trees grow of their own accord. They're often found at the edge of mangroves and among other wild plants and planted ones like cacao, banana, cassava, and coconut. Harvesting can be dangerous—the trees can reach one hundred feet tall, and sometimes have snakes living in their tops.

Dendê is so embedded in Bahia, that it even shows up in slang, says Elmo Alves, a sous chef and historian who teaches at the culinary school of the Serviço Nacional de Aprendizagem Comercial in Salvador. "You might say, 'Ah, that girl has dendê,'" he says. "That means she has a certain strength, a certain energy. She has presence, Bahia-ness."

In Bahia, there's a whole group of traditional Afro-Brazilian foods called *comidas de azeite*. They all have dendê oil in common. These dishes aren't just for people, but are also for the gods. Candomblé, a Brazilian religion with West African roots, was founded by former slaves in Bahia. A pantheon of gods and goddesses, called *orixás*, are worshipped, and each one has its favorite foods. Almost all of the orixás eat dendê oil, says Juveni Jovelino, the spiritual leader of Kaonge, a community founded by escaped slaves, including her great-grandfather. "It is the base of everything, and it comes from our ancestors."

Alves says it's this religious dimension that has helped preserve Bahia's food traditions. "Bahian food isn't just an everyday food," he says. "It's a cuisine that's a religious practice." Alves is a devotee of Omolú, a god associated with sickness and health, mystery, and ancestry—and also popcorn and black beans stewed in dendê oil.

One of the most popular of these sacred dishes is *acarajé,* a bean fritter fried in dendê oil that's sold on street corners, plazas, outside schools and offices—everywhere. Acarajé gets its name from a Nigerian snack called *akara*. In Bahia, many enslaved women bought their freedom selling acarajé in streets. They're known as *Baianas*.

Mary de Jesus is a third-generation acarajé seller in Salvador. Baianas are known for their baroque and beautiful clothing. (Carmen Miranda's costume was a tarted-up take on Baiana style.) Mary is particularly resplendent. When we meet, she's wearing a bright striped turban, piles of long, beaded necklaces (each one symbolizes a god), and a long ruffled skirt over petticoats that exaggerate her hips by six inches on each side. She has shimmery gold and salmon eye shadows to the brow, and perfect red lipstick.

In a wok-like pan over a gas burner,

Mary is making acarajés. "You can't fry an acarajé in soy oil or any other oil, because then it won't be an acarajé," she says. Each morning, she puts half a raw onion in the oil for flavoring; by late afternoon it's black and looks like a like a dead peony. To make the fritter, she explains, you soak black-eyed peas whose skins have been removed. Then, without cooking the beans, you grind them into a paste that's mixed with minced raw onion and salt. Stir it with big, round motions to get air into the batter, then drop it by the spoonful into dendê oil and fry it to a deep orange-brown.

Once pulled from the oil, the fritter is split in two, then filled with dried smoked shrimp, one smear of a green paste made from okra and dendê, and another of a red one made from dendê and manioc. Hot peppers and tomatoes finish it off. On the street, acarajé are fist-sized and served in squares of paper. As soon as I bite into of one of Mary's acarajés, a bony cat appears at my feet. The fritter is wonderfully crunchy on the outside, and the inside is white with a cake-like crumb. The shrimp are salty and dense with crunchy skins. The hot, vinegary peppers sting my lips.

Most Baianas are devotees of Iansã, the passionate and sensual goddess of wind and lightning. But they offer the first acarajé of each batch to Exú, the trickster god of the crossroads, who facilitates communication between humans and the gods. Exú's exacting and controversial; some Christians associate him with the devil, though devotees say he encompasses both good and evil. Evangelical Christianity has gained a lot of ground in Brazil in recent years, and some preachers teach that Candomblé is devil-worship. Some converted Baianas (or evangelicals who entered the trade) began selling acarajé under the name *bolinhos de Jesus,* which translates infelicitously to "little Jesus balls."

"They used to say that acarajés belonged to the devil," explains Solange

dos Santos, who's been selling acarajés for more than thirty years. "Now some of them are selling it."

The acarajés served in Candomblé houses are smaller than the street version, about the size of an apricot. I got the chance to try one at the Ilê Axé Opô Afonjá *terreiro,* in Salvador. The terreiro is a temple—more of a compound, really—with a house devoted to each orixá and even a public school. Tonight, there's a ceremony for Oxóssi, a hunter associated with prosperity and abundance.

I hear the terriero before I see it. Firecrackers are going off overhead and there are drums coming from inside. I take a seat behind an altar of fresh fruit—it's hot and the air is thick with the smell of passion fruit and papaya and a trace of saltpeter. A handful of people are dancing in front of a group of drummers. Not long after we arrive, the dancers disappear and people start passing big trays piled with clay plates of food. This holy meal is called the *ajeum.* My plate is heaped with bits of different foods, each associated with an orixá. Iansã's acarajé is there, a little golden football. There are large, chewy kernels of corn for Oxóssi; an okra-and-palm-oil dish called *amalá* for Xangô, the god of thunder and lightning; and cassava

flour fried in dendê oil for Exú.

After the meal, the dancers reemerge wearing fantastic costumes. They are lending their bodies to the orixás tonight. Three are dressed as Oxóssi—two women and a man. The women wear bell-shaped princess skirts and beads, but also vests made of skins and olive scout hats. The man has a yellow fur tail swinging from the side of his hat and a slightly mangy-looking vest. He has an intense, twitchy way of dancing, often just pacing at the edge of the crowd. The dancers come near the sidelines and the people hold up their palms to them, to show respect and also to absorb *axé,* or life-force. When the male Oxóssi beelines toward a group of people near me, one big young guy tips over in a dead faint and another woman crumples and starts sobbing and muttering.

The dancers look feverish and their eyes stay cast down. They are being cared for tenderly by members of the terriero. One of the Oxóssis, an older woman, does a low swooping dance. Every time she looks like she might tip over, someone materializes from the sidelines and steadies her by the elbow. There's a bench near me where the dancers rest. Their caretakers use white cloths to dry their brows and then gingerly lift their coils of necklaces and blot sweat from their necks and shoulders. Finally, the terreiro's leader, a ninety-year-old woman known as Mãe Stella, takes her leave, and the ceremony is over. People descend on the fruit altar, grabbing pieces for themselves and filling trays to take to the people in the room's farther reaches. A man shoos me toward the altar, telling me to go and take some for myself. "Eat it for breakfast tomorrow," someone tells me. "It's full of axé."

About a thousand miles northwest of Bahia, in the state of Pará, Brazil's been working to open a new frontier for palm-oil production. Raymundo Fernandez Nascimento de Almeida, who goes by Junior, is a family farmer who recently converted to

dendê production. He takes me on a tour of his plantings, and I'm struck by how different these trees look. While the trees that grow semi-wild in Bahia are tall and Seussian, these are stockier and all top. They look like someone took a regular, tall palm tree and buried it up to its neck in the dirt.

Junior is tall and lean with a long, narrow face, whose skin looks stretched tight over his cheekbones. He's wearing a T-shirt from Sodexo, the gigantic French food-services company. He tells me that all this land was once cassava fields. But over the last fifteen years, some sort of disease started making the cassava roots rot in the ground. Now there are no other crops growing among the palm trees—just crisp grass.

Junior doesn't eat dendê oil—it's not popular in Pará—and, when representatives from Archer Daniels Midland started showing up in his town about five years ago, he didn't know much about the company, except that it was "a multinational." ADM is headquartered in Chicago, and it's one of the biggest food-processing companies in the world. It makes vegetable oils, corn syrup, biodiesel, and lots of other products. Now, it's setting up some plantations and also recruiting family farmers to grow palm.

This was just one small part of a big push to make northern Brazil a hub for producing palm oil. There were already some palm operations in the state, and the number of acres planted grew steadily in the 2000s. But in 2010, the federal government, along with some energy and food companies, launched an aggressive plan. The goal was to turn Pará into a big producer of biofuel made from palm oil.

One of the selling points was a plan to help family farmers convert to palm production. In 2010, former president Luiz Inácio Lula da Silva climbed on a platform in the town of Tomé-Açu to announce that the government would

invest millions of dollars to push palm oil expansion. "We are starting a revolution in this region," he said. The government pledged to develop up to 12.3 million acres of land in the Amazon region that it deemed ideal for palm oil production. (There are about 40.6 million acres of oil palm worldwide). Months earlier, Brazil's state-run oil company committed to opening a palm-oil processing plant in the state, and a huge mining company invested in a palm-oil company to make biofuel. After describing how the government was going to help small farmers get in on the action, Lula had even convinced himself: "Even *I'm* going to want to plant palm," he said.

The expansion plan raised many red flags. Pará's been losing forest faster than other states in the Brazilian Amazon, much of it due to illegal logging and agriculture (including some of the palm plantations planted before 2010). But Brazil's new plan aimed to avoid the problems that had plagued the industry elsewhere. The new plan specified that palm could

only be planted on land that was already abandoned and degraded—rainforest that had been cleared years ago for cattle or sugarcane, for example. Federal law requires landowners in Pará to keep half of their land in forest, or replant forest if it's already gone. While the details vary a bit depending on the company, farmers would sign twenty-five-year contracts to produce dendê for a company. In exchange, the company would teach the farmers to grow dendê and buy the fruit. The government, for its part, would lend small farmers the money they needed to plant about twenty-five acres of dendê. In many cases, it would also help farmers get legal titles to land—a huge deal in Brazil where lots of farmers work land that they don't have an official title to. Most of the family farmers growing dendê have about sixty-two acres of land, half of which has to be kept in forestland or replanted if it's already been deforested.

Of course, working with small farmers wasn't an entirely altruistic move for the companies; it helped some of them access

government subsidies and incentives, and it let them expand their operations at little cost to themselves. Plus, dealing with family farmers makes the companies look good—crucial for huge and powerful entities planting one of the world's most notoriously destructive crops in one of the most ecologically important regions in the world.

Many environmentalists were cautiously optimistic. Rhett Butler, writing in *Yale Environment 360*, spelled out some of the reasons: Most of the deforested land in Pará is degraded cattle pasture, and planting palm could provide ranchers with an alternative to cutting down more trees. Palm sequesters more carbon than pasture, and could also help reestablish the region's hydrological cycles that were disrupted by deforestation, which would in turn reduce drought. And, if Brazil could become a model for how palm oil could be produced sustainably, it could pressure producers elsewhere to change their ways. One company, Agropalma, was certified as sustainable in 2011 and had its operations praised by Greenpeace as "a blueprint" for responsible production.

To Junior, it seemed a good option, too: "I thought it was interesting, because it's an income source over a long period of time. Up until now, there hasn't been another crop that would offer us these conditions. I decided to do it."

Between 2011 and 2014, the amount of oil palm planted in Pará doubled, according to the Center for International Forestry Research (CIFOR). To get a sense of the scale, I take a drive through the main palm-growing region with Elielson Pereira da Silva, who works for an agricultural workers' association called Federação dos Trabalhadores na Agricultura do Estado do Pará. We drive down dusty washboard roads that part seas of palm. Most of the vehicles on the road are tanker trucks hauling palm oil. We pass occasional clusters of houses; most have an evangelical church. "The gospel of prosperity," da Silva says.

It's still way too soon to say whether or not Brazil's plans for palm-oil expansion in Pará will live up to their promise. There's been a lot of chaos in the six years since the biofuel plan was announced here. The country's fallen into an economic crisis. There's been a huge political corruption scandal and impeachment proceedings have begun for the current president. In September, Brazil's currency, the *real,* fell to its lowest value since it was introduced twenty years ago.

Before our trip, da Silva told me he didn't want to "demonize" palm oil. "But just as you can't demonize it, you can't sanctify it either," he said. Da Silva's been tracking the industry's growth and says a series of "worrying questions" have emerged. He's concerned that a lot of small farmers signed contracts without entirely comprehending what it could mean to dedicate most of their land to a single crop for twenty-five years and to yoke themselves to the same big company for the duration. Da Silva questions why the government is incentivizing monocultures. A more diversified "agroforestry" approach, like the mixed groves in Bahia, would be good for the environment, and it would also mean farmers could grow more food for themselves instead of depending on a cash crop. The amount that farmers are paid for their palm is affected by global forces that are far out of their control.

Moreover, despite the promise to make clean energy from palm oil, none of the palm oil produced in Pará is being made into biofuel. "I think that was just a bit of marketing on the part of the government," Leonardo Dutra, a field coordinator who works with ADM, told me with a chuckle. His boss, Diego Di Martino, explains it this way: "It's a nice ecological idea to make green fuel. But it doesn't work that way." The food and cosmetics industries pay

much more than the biodiesel market. "We don't use a single drop of palm oil for biodiesel in Brazil," Di Martino says.

But new research does suggest that that the Brazilian government's restrictions on where dendê can be planted seem to be working. In a recent report evaluating palm production in Pará, CIFOR researchers wrote, "Early evidence appears to suggest that these initiatives have contributed to ameliorating the negative social and environmental risks that have long characterized the crop's expansion in Southeast Asia." The recent expansion of palm plantings, the researchers found, has occurred on already deforested land and does not appear to be driving deforestation.

That doesn't mean there haven't been any problems. Companies haven't contracted with as many family farmers as they'd initially planned to, the researchers found. Slave labor persists in Brazil, and there have been at least two cases of palm-oil producers using slaves. One of them was the deputy mayor of one of the major palm-producing towns, Moju, who grew palm for Agropalma. The company has since terminated the contract with the deputy mayor. An indigenous group is suing another palm-oil company for allegedly using the pesticides endosulfan and DDT, which they say have harmed their crops, animals, and health. And there have been a handful of conflicts between some companies that have illegitimately gotten title to and started operating on land that has long been occupied by descendants of escaped slaves (though courts ruled in favor of the communities).

As for the larger promise—that Pará would become an important palm-producing region and even a model for the industry—it still seems a long way off. After an initial frenzy, the sector started to stagnate in 2014, according to the CIFOR paper, and many companies have scaled back their expansion plans, for now at least. The researchers say that,

among other factors, Brazil's comparatively stringent environmental and labor laws—the ones that made Pará's palm-oil expansion seem like it might not be such a bad thing—may mean that palm oil from Pará just can't compete in the global marketplace.

But for Junior, things are going pretty well. He planted his trees in 2012 and started harvesting last year. In his field, there are bunches of dendê fruit all over the palms, tucked between the fronds. The fruit is smaller than the fruit Santos used to make oil in Bahia, but it's a variety that produces more oil and has smaller seeds. Junior's already harvesting more than he expected—he's averaging four or five tons every ten days. He's already earning enough from the dendê for the family to live on, along with the pensions from his grandmother and mother, who live with them. But drought looms: it hasn't rained in a hundred days, and the plants and people are suffering. Most farmers don't have any way to water. One neighbor's dendê fields caught on fire. "He came to me and he cried," Junior says. "He doesn't have any other way to make a living." The fields will recover, but it will take two years.

At lunch with Junior's family, we eat salty fried fish and big bowls of acai, another fruit of a palm. Junior says he tries not to get his hopes up too much about the future. "I can't predict," he says. "We hope this will be good for us. But nothing's ever 100 percent."

After we leave Junior, we stop at an intersection, so Dutra from ADM can get cell-phone reception. In Bahia, people often leave offerings at crossroads for Exú. Here at this red-dirt junction, I see a cluster of dendê fruit. It appears to have been carefully placed, and the fruit is perfect, just dusted with dirt. It probably fell from an ADM truck, but I can't help but think it looks like an entreaty for Exú to open the way. **LP**

CRE
WA

BY
MADHUR JAFFREY

ILLUSTRATIONS BY
MADDIE EDGAR

PETROS

It is the end of a glorious summer's day in Crete. The wind has picked up. Whitecaps are racing each other in the sea. It is now quite chilly and getting dark. As I pull my shawl closer, I think of something that my companion, Petros Kaplatzis, a fisherman from Sfakia in southwestern Crete, told me.

"Good weather catches fish," Petros said, his eyes holding mine with a mesmerizing stillness, "the fisherman only thinks he is catching them." Winds had kept Petros from going out on his boat for the past seven days. On such blustery days, he could put his nets down in one place and they could soon end up in another one entirely. He has a wife and two children to feed. Would tomorrow be any different?

I am thinking of Petros's words, watching the day end while sitting by the water in the northern resort town of Hersonissos, eating octopus. The restaurant, Saradari, is terraced upward from the sea, with tented pavilions on the green grass, little and big encampments loosely separating groups of diners from one another.

We have already dined leisurely on *gavros*—delicate little fish split open, deboned, "cooked" briefly in lemon juice and sea salt, and then dressed with olive oil—and cuttlefish cooked in their own ink and red wine. Grilled squid served over a split-pea purée, fried anchovies, and *barbounia*,

fried red mullet, are to follow. In between are two octopus courses: one a large grilled tentacle (*arm* or *limb* would be more accurate) served with roasted and puréed eggplant and the other a delightful, hand-rolled, fresh pasta cooked in octopus broth and dotted with garlicky slices of octopus and salami from the island of Lefkada.

Petros had told me about the weather and the fish and the relationship between man and the sea when we were sitting in a café on the port side of Heraklion, the capital city, drinking coffee. Facing us were medieval Venetian fortifications, built as a solid seawall. "Look beyond them to the island of Dia, just to the north. That was once a ferocious sea monster. Zeus turned it into a rock." He seemed to believe what he was telling me.

Petros often fished in bays around Dia. One day, sonar indicated that there was a big fish on the line. But it was inside an ancient jar. This is a particularly Greek hazard. By law, all fishermen, on pain of going to jail, have to take such jars to the museum. The museum has so many ancient jars, it offers only sighs of mild boredom when they are brought in. The fisherman is caught in the middle, filling out paperwork.

Paperwork of a different stripe burdens all Cretan fishermen today: I have arrived in the middle of the Greek financial crisis. Deep uncertainty clouds the island. What will the prime minister, Alexis Tsipras, be able to work out? All banks are closed. Tourists can use their credit cards freely but locals can only withdraw sixty euros a day.

There was a time when Petros had an assistant whom he paid 3,000 euros a day. He himself was making 15,000 euros a day catching lobsters. That was ten years ago. The lobsters are mostly fished out. Now Petros prepares his nets and fishing line alone, and he fishes alone.

Gas prices are high, and his insurance has suddenly gone up fourfold; he cannot take his boat out too often. Poisonous rabbitfish from the Red Sea have invaded the Mediterranean. They eat all other fish and grow large. Meanwhile, dolphins punch holes in his nets, which take him a month to repair but can be destroyed again in a minute.

But now, sitting in the harbor and slowly sipping his coffee, Petros is taking the long view,

87

hoping that winter will bring him some squid, which he will catch by dropping nets in bays where they are known to live. One net load can collect 330 pounds. Stuffed, stewed, fried, or grilled, they are very popular with Cretans, particularly at Lent.

BLOBLOS

Seafood has been elemental to Cretan life since antiquity. There is a sprawling palace at Knossos with giant tapered pillars painted black and red. The ruling class wore clothing dyed a royal purple from the hard-to-obtain hypobranchial glands of the rare murex gastropod; murals in the queen's room display dolphins and sea urchins, and charming octopus patterns were painted on clay bathtubs. Bronze spears and metal fishhooks have been found at Gournia, an excavation site in Mirabello Bay.

In Crete, parents urge their children into the water at a very early age, almost as ducks do their ducklings. They learn which rock they should swim to in order to pull off the freshest shellfish for instant feasts. They are told to pick sea urchins when the moon is full (otherwise they won't be full themselves) and harvest only those with a green, red, or purple "eye." Black "eyes" must be discarded. They know how to crack open these spiny creatures. Some they eat right away; the rest they carry home in bags to be eaten later, dressed with a little seawater, olive oil, and lemon juice. They also know that whole red mullet, whether fried or grilled, need their spines removed for easy eating. This is best done by pressing down on the top fin as the fish lies on the plate. Most of the skeletal structure can then be pulled away.

Manolis Voutsalas, commonly known as Bloblos, is an award-winning diver, a fisherman, and a player of many other parts. His grandmother was from Kalymnos, and most of his male relatives were sponge divers. I met him in the company of a group of friends he invited to a tavern by the sea in Heraklion. It is a brief period of quiet for him before he takes off with Jean-Michel Cousteau on his boat, a trip that will include both diving for shipwrecks and cooking. He is a mean cook.

He has brought with him a very large *sfirida* (grouper), weighing about thirteen pounds, which has been halved laterally. Both halves, under his instructions, are seasoned only with sea salt—the salt releases the liquids inside the fish and readies it for grilling, he explains.

While we wait, we are regaled with fish stories, offered plates of sea urchins, bread for dipping into the sea-urchin sauce, and shot upon shot of *raki*, a clear, dangerously strong liqueur made from grape pomace.

Bloblos has also brought with him a large sack of green almonds, which are in season. He is cracking them open with a pair of tongue-and-groove pliers, peeling each almond himself and passing them on to the dozen or so diners. The fish arrives on two platters. It smells of the sea. Each half is dressed with olive oil and lemon, and we are encouraged to tear into it with our hands. The skin is crisp and delicious, the flesh tender and glistening, the parts between the large bones satiny and glorious. Even the slightly blackened tail is devoured with gusto. The fried liver, considered a delicacy, arrives by itself. Lime is squeezed on it and it is carefully portioned out. This is easily the best grilled fish I have ever eaten.

Bloblos has speared this fish with a harpoon. He has a personal record of staying underwater without oxygen for four minutes and fifteen seconds—he has never smoked. (He dives with oxygen tanks, too. Decompression problems on one trip caused him six months of paralysis and an all-too-slow recovery, but he carries on.) He understands his fish. Groupers, he says, go into individual holes in the seabed. If he harpoons a grouper and then returns to the same hole, he is likely to find the hole occupied by a grouper

89

of exactly the same size. He has speared groupers weighing up to forty-four pounds.

Sometimes a grouper will share a hole with an octopus, he tells me. One goes out and the other comes in. Since both make good eating, Bloblos keeps a watchful eye on the hole. He has a trick for catching an octopus. Other fishermen use boxy traps baited with cooked chicken or even cooked octopus in order to catch these slippery creatures. Bloblos reaches with his hand and gently pulls it out. He then lets it go but does not let it get too far. He catches it again and lets it go again. After a few rounds of seduction, the octopus becomes tame and can be handled easily.

KAKAVIA

Before my trip, I'd read and heard about a Cretan soup of fish and vegetables called *kakavia*. Once in Crete, I learned that there are many versions of the soup, but that the best one is to be found at the seaside tavern on a cliff, Delfini, in Linoperamata, not far from Heraklion. It must be ordered in advance, which my hosts, the Marouda family, did for me. As I wanted to watch the soup being prepared, my hosts introduced me to the chefs and owners, Antonis and his wife, Katerina, who now lead me into their kitchen.

Half of a nine-pound grouper, cut laterally, is the fish to be used for the soup. It was caught on the family's own fishing line, fitted out with thousands of secondary lines, each ending in a hook. Each hook was baited with cooked octopus. All this painstaking work was done by Vasilis, Antonis and Katerina's son. Sometimes a live octopus gets caught and devours the groupers near it. That is par for the course.

Antonis and Katerina quarter large potatoes—larger than most Idahoes—and arrange them to line a large pot, cut side up. "This way they won't stick," they tell me. On top of this goes a layer of quartered zucchini, chunky carrot pieces, sliced celery, and onions. The fish is cut into large chunks, too. The fins, head, and tail are layered inside first and topped with the rest of the fish. Water, then olive oil, grated tomato, and salt follow. The pot boils for thirty or forty minutes before lemon juice is added and the pot is shaken to mix it in. As the soup cooks, my hosts offer the popular Cretan preprandial combination: shots of raki and slices of crisp cucumber from their farm, sprinkled with sea salt.

All the while, some insane miracle is taking place in the kakavia pot. Antonis lifts the lid, and picks up the fish pieces with a slotted spoon. They are still intact. He lays them out in a large platter. Next to them he places the carrots, the zucchini, and the potatoes. The liquid is strained into a large bowl. The oil and lemon juice have, perhaps with the help of the potatoes and the gelatin from the fish, been forced to cohere and form a sauce that holds together.

We sit by the windows, looking down over the high cliff at the dark sea. First the soup is ladled into our bowls, to which we add as much of the fish and vegetables as we like. We squeeze lemon juice over the top, and it is one of the best fish stews I have eaten, the kind of dish I could have for my dinner every day. But it is not the only thing at the table: there is an exquisite dolma in the form of stuffed zucchini flowers, *horta* (the greens of the season), grilled octopus, sea urchin, and baby cuttlefish cooked in its own ink. Raki and wine flow freely.

I ask my kind hosts why, even in a time of great insecurity, with devastating financial and political crises roiling just beneath the surface, they never let me see a single frown of anxiety. That is the Cretan way, they say. It is important to them that, for their guests, every day is just another perfect summer's day in Crete. 🍑

91

Orderly Disordered Eating

BY LUCAS PETERSON

ILLUSTRATIONS BY ELEANOR DAVIS

"You were in the choir at Interlochen," said my mom, when I asked her what she remembered about the summer between my freshman and sophomore years of high school. "You were in the choir, remember? And you were standing on the risers, and I think you fainted and fell off or something."

Yes, of course I remember, but I don't remember you saying anything to me about it afterward. Do you also remember that I lost a ton of weight that summer?

"Well, yes," she said, starting to sound a little apprehensive. "We all noticed you'd slimmed down a lot. And I remember asking your dad if he thought we should be concerned."

And were you?

"Of course." She paused. "But we didn't think you had, like, an eating disorder or anything. We all have weird food things as kids; I remember one summer I decided I'd only eat carrots, and the soles of my feet started to turn orange. It's just part of growing up."

The summer before I went into third grade, my parents thought it would be nice for me to spend some one-on-one time with my Pau Pau, my mom's mom. We flew from LAX and went on a long trip together around Hong Kong, where she's from, and Taiwan. She was (and still is) an accomplished, caring woman and an easy traveler—low maintenance and rarely ruffled by unexpected events or inconveniences. And over the course of the trip, she was as accommodating as she could be to a slightly spoiled child who found a number of things unsatisfactory.

It was my first trip to Asia, and I had a few complaints. They mostly involved the bathrooms we encountered (squat toilets? No thanks, I'll hold it in!) and the food I was presented while visiting various old friends and family in that part of the world. I just couldn't wrap my head around it: Why was everything so slick and goopy? Why were so many acceptable foods ruined by the addition of something weird-tasting, e.g., a bunch of hot squid thrown onto some perfectly good noodles, or pork stuffed into a nice, plain steamed *bao*? The fact that no one ate things like cheese or breakfast cereal was pure lunacy. And the way things smelled while we were walking down the street made me want to retch: a mixture of raw meat, urine, rotting vegetables, and car exhaust.

After three weeks, Pau Pau was reaching the end of her tether. We were about to head to a somewhat important banquet commemorating the birthday of an older auntie, and she was looking to bargain. If I could behave, she promised, as soon as we got back to America, she would let me have all the McDonald's I wanted. I'm sorry—did you say *all the McDonald's I wanted*? Yes, she said, but no more complaining the rest of the trip. Could I do it? There was a McDonald's less than a

half mile away from Pau Pau's house in Encino. When we finally, finally came back to LA, I was ready to make her stick to her promise. I had one week before my parents came to pick me up. We walked to McDonald's every day, sometimes more than once a day, and, as promised, I got whatever I wanted. That was usually a Happy Meal, or sometimes just fries, or sometimes just the fries out of the Happy Meal. The fries, as everyone knows, are the best thing about McDonald's: hot, salty, fried in beef tallow (at least they were in the eighties), and with a perfect ratio of stubby, crunchy fries to long, slack, soft ones.

I had had a normal little kid's body up until that point. But that year, I started getting chubby. Food, especially junk food, felt special: something I could enjoy alone after school and when my parents were at work. Something that made me feel better when I was sad, or lonely, or feeling rejected. My mom was a brilliant cook and fed people great food, and those people loved her for it. I thought I would try to apply that to my own life.

There was a small general store called Blase's, on Lake Street near my elementary school. I'd go there in the mornings and spend my allowance money on various snacks and treats: Doritos, Funyuns, different flavors of Now & Laters, Big League Chew, and long, Slim Jim–esque sticks of chewing gum called Bub's Daddy. I'd walk the two blocks over to school with a brown paper bag full of candy, gnawing on some Alexander the Grapes along the way. Once at school, I'd go over to the gravel field and we'd play a game: I (or whichever kid had bought candy that day) would stand thirty or so feet away from a big group of kids. I would throw a fistful of candy as high as I could into the air, and the group would fight over the bounty. We'd repeat this until the candy was gone. It wasn't much of a game, but it was a win-win for everyone involved: kids would get candy, and I would get temporary attention and

a spike in popularity with the kids who played, sometimes even the very popular and athletic kids. The friendships never lasted long, and eventually, I ran out of money (I took to stealing money from my mom's purse and soon got busted for that).

In the meantime, I kept gaining weight. I was a little husky by the end of grade school, but by the time junior high rolled around, I was flat-out chunky. And, entering a new school with kids who were fully in the throes of puberty, I really paid attention to my appearance for the first time. I didn't like what I saw: big cheeks, round face, and a double chin. There was a roll of fat on each side of my chest, where my arm met my armpit. I had a big tummy and could grab big handfuls of fat on my stomach and sides. My torso was shaped like a piece of candy corn.

It dawned on me for the first time that I hated my body. Kids called me fat. Girls did not pay attention to me. A particularly nasty kid named Tim would punch me in the stomach and call me "lard-ass" and "faggot." I did everything to avoid situations that involved going shirtless. "Shirts versus skins" were the three deadliest words in the English language. My parents signed me up for the local swim team in an effort to get me moving in a way that didn't entail hand-eye coordination. I would sooner have died than jam myself into a Speedo. I pretended to go to practice for months: I would take my suit and towel and walk out the door and down the street, toward the pool. I would go to the library instead, and get my suit and towel wet in the water fountain before coming home.

After school, I would eat and watch TV. I was frequently unsupervised until my parents came home in the evening. We didn't keep junk food at the house, so I'd order a pizza from Domino's. I would eat the entire thing—thin, sweet sauce; insubstantial cheese; airy, chewy crust—and hide the empty boxes on our back porch. At night, I'd transfer them to the garbage in the alley. Sometimes I would put them in the neighbor's garbage to be extra sneaky. On days I didn't get a pizza, I would stop by this lousy diner, sit alone at the counter, and eat a pound of steak fries: thick, oily, and scalding hot, sitting on a sheet of wax paper in a brown or red plastic basket.

I was closing in on two hundred pounds when I entered high school. I hated myself for eating too much, and I didn't want anyone to see my body. I especially hated going to school. A kid named Aaron would come up to my desk and whisper to me that I was fat and that he'd fucked my mom last night. A sophomore named Jon in my world history class would torment me when the teacher stepped out. Mr. Weinberg, who was a great teacher and a very nice man, left the room a lot, for whatever reason. When he did, Jon's face would positively light up. "What are you gonna do, egg roll?" Jon would yell to me from his seat. "You can't run, and you're too fat to hide!" Uncomfortable titters came from my classmates at first, but their response eventually settled into light, familiar laughter.

I never said a word back to him—he was taller and stronger than I was—and despite the frequency of this happening, I always felt totally blindsided. I would feebly try to think of comebacks, but they would never come in time. *Should I make fun of how skinny he is? No, that doesn't make sense. Should I go racial? He went racial with me. He's black. Is that okay? No, no, that's probably not okay.* By that point, it was too late to respond; Mr. Weinberg had returned. Plus, I thought, he was right: I was fat.

At lunch, I supplemented my parentally made healthy lunch with two items from the school cafeteria: pizza puffs— deep-fried, fist-sized pockets of tasteless white cheese and pet-food-grade meat—and chocolate chip cookies. The cookies at Oak Park and River Forest High School were pornographically greasy: they shimmered under the fluorescent lights of the cafeteria. The paper plates they were served on were soaked through with fat and completely translucent. The cookie couldn't be lifted off the plate, as it had no structural integrity: it had to be pulled apart in weak, lazy strips. Eating it required no chewing: once you'd put a piece in your mouth, it slowly slid down your throat. It was sweet, sticky, and fatty: otherworldly in its deliciousness and also simultaneously the pinnacle of horrendous, unctuous junk food. It was so, so good. And I ate so, so many of them.

My parents tried to help me, in the kindest, most unobtrusive way possible. My mom, in particular, understood, as she had struggled with her weight and spent a lot of my childhood cycling through various diets. The hot guru of the moment was Covert Bailey (think: younger, less cool Jack LaLanne), who'd written a book called *Fit or Fat?* Bailey's advice to engage in consistent, varied exercise made good sense. His take on diet did not: he was among the many dieticians and gurus of the era that promoted a philosophy of, *If you want less fat on you, put less fat in you.* Meaning, the key to weight loss was simply incessant exercise and foods low in fat. That could mean a number of things: broccoli is low in fat, as are apples, chicken breast, and lettuce. Also: pastas, breads, Skittles, Twizzlers, and Fun Dip.

I started going to an aerobics class, but I also pounded pasta and candy like nobody's business, safe in the assumption that, since they were low-fat foods, I would quickly be losing weight. Nabisco came out with a horrible line of ostensibly "healthy" cookies called SnackWell's; I would ravage box after box of their devil's-food-cake cookies and be puzzled when I stepped on the scale and found that I had actually gained weight from the week before. *These are fat-free cookies,* I would think to myself. *What the fuck?*

I used to go to this allergy doctor named Dr. Swartz who would give me injections to help me deal with my hay fever. Sometimes I would steal empty syringes from his office and bring them

home with me. One time, up in my room, with the door closed, I took one out, uncapped it, and jabbed it into my belly. I remember being surprised that it didn't hurt. With the needle stuck in my gut, I pulled up the plunger, thinking I could suck some fat out and do a little home liposuction. Nothing came out.

I went to sleepaway summer camp for the first and only time during the summer between my freshman and sophomore years of high school. The camp was located at the Interlochen Center for the Arts, a sprawling 1,200-acre campus in the northern Michigan woods, about fifteen miles from the nearest town, Traverse City (if Michigan is a mitten, Traverse City is on the tip of the pinkie finger). Two thousand kids from all over the world descended for eight weeks to focus on music, theater, dance, creative writing, and visual arts.

The first thing I noticed was that everyone there was really fucking good at music. There was a South American phenom named Rodolfo who could blast through Beethoven's Piano Concerto in C minor. I was at the camp for piano, too, and my teacher, an old Croatian woman of cartoonish austerity, was severely unimpressed by my skill. The singers at Interlochen were especially intimidating: everyone sang with vibrato and could

hit—and sustain—outrageously high notes. An older boy named Jason was a fantastic comedian and had leads in the musical, *Anything Goes,* and in the operetta, *The Pirates of Penzance*. Norah Jones and Josh Groban would attend camp in upcoming years. Interlochen was for kids who wanted to go pro—kids more talented and more serious than I was.

Camp was, for the most part, how I imagined camp would be. There was the usual pecking order, even if the bullying was pretty tame compared to things that happened at home. We were, after all, at an *art* camp—even the mean kids still sang opera. On our bathroom stall doors, instead of suggestive poetry or girls' phone numbers, kids scrawled in ballpoint pen: PLEASE DO NOT APPLAUD BETWEEN MOVEMENTS. Still, I wasn't making friends easily, and I felt vastly inferior as a musician. So I decided that losing weight would be my activity. I would be better at losing weight than Rodolfo was at piano, or Jason was at musical theater. I would shed these fat cheeks and fat stomach once and for all. I would resist the pasta and cereal with monastic discipline. It wouldn't be *too* hard, I thought—the food was fairly military in its predictability and quality, so I wouldn't be missing out on much. I just needed to make a plan and stick to it.

When I went to the cafeteria with kids from my cabin,

I wouldn't stay; I'd run in and grab a couple pieces of fruit and a few crackers. That had the additional benefit of not having to find a group of people to sit with. I would take a few oranges and eat them while walking around, shedding the peels on the cool, pine-needle-covered ground as I went. I ate a countless number of oranges that summer. And I drank water. Whenever I got hungry, I would drink water until my stomach was full. I gradually stopped going to meals entirely.

It was working. After a couple weeks, my clothes felt a little looser. I could hitch my belt one notch more than I used to. There were hunger pangs, and those could get pretty killer, especially at night. But I drank water to alleviate them, and we'd occasionally have snacks at night in the cabin. They were always greasy or sugary, pizza or s'mores and the like. I'd want to stuff my face, but I held the line and fought the desire. I imagined eating and throwing up the food, but dismissed that behavior as an illness. What I was doing, dieting, was fine. If you made yourself vomit, that meant something very serious.

Eating-disorder resources weren't widely accessible in the early nineties, especially for boys. I certainly don't remember anyone ever bringing it up at school or among my peer group. Even today, most assessment tests are skewed for women. This is understandable—by all accounts, women and young girls are the most affected. On the website of the National Eating Disorders Association, in order to find any kind of information about how eating disorders affect men and boys, you have to go over to the menu and scroll to where it says DIVERSITY ISSUES, subheading MALES.

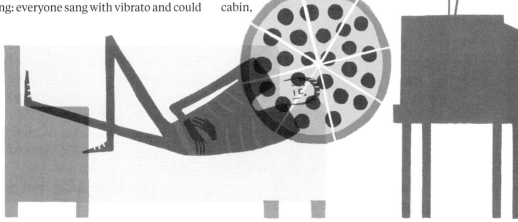

"Prevalence figures for males with eating disorders (ED) are somewhat elusive," the site confesses. "In the past, ED have been characterized as 'women's problems' and men have been stigmatized from coming forward or have been unaware that they could have an ED." When you dig a little, though, there are some stats for men, though the stats are confusing and vary wildly depending on the source. The NEDA maintains that 90 to 95 percent of anorexia sufferers are female. The National Institute of Mental Health site estimates that 2.5 times more women are affected than men. These statistics, like all statistics, rely on accurate reporting. And if you'd approached me with a survey that summer at camp, I certainly would have checked the "No" box under "Do you have an eating disorder?"

If you had asked me about eating disorders, I would have talked to you about two things: One was an old episode of *St. Elsewhere* where this woman almost dies force-feeding herself chocolate from a caulking gun. The other would have been Karen Carpenter. That, to my mind, was what having an eating disorder was: an acutely violent relationship with food that quickly and inevitably led to death. I wasn't dying, and what I was doing had a *purpose*. I had made a choice to do what I was doing, and I had control over it. I didn't need to be crazy thin, I just wanted to shed some excess weight. I knew I couldn't not-eat forever. I felt like I had gone from a life of secret, shameful eating to a life of secret, shameful not-eating. What I was doing wasn't healthy; I knew that. But I was invested in seeing my plan through, at having success and achieving my goal, and at not having to write off my past weeks of effort as unhealthy or a waste of time. I'd do it until I didn't see a fat kid in the mirror anymore. An eating disorder was fraught and dramatic, and I never would have admitted to having one—the reality was, of course, that I did.

And it wasn't dramatic or exciting, either: it was lonely, slow, and boring.

By week six or seven, I was very noticeably thinner. I couldn't really see it, but my pants were falling down now, so I definitely knew I was losing weight. I'd look at myself in the mirror with mixed feelings: I was smaller than I had been, to be sure, but I still had belly fat. I hadn't transformed into an Adonis-like physical specimen. I was still shaped like myself, but there was less of me. I couldn't let myself stop. The few times I sat down in the cafeteria to try to eat actual food, like a plate of pasta, my stomach swelled after the first couple of bites and I couldn't eat any more. Hunger pangs certainly gnawed, but I stuck to my normal routine: run in quickly, grab some oranges and a couple crackers before I could be seen, and run out. One time while doing this I almost knocked over Yo-Yo Ma. He could not have been nicer about it. I munched on a tart, sweet orange during my walk back to the boys' cabins.

Losing weight was the payoff, and it was really satisfying. It felt like progress, and all I wanted was to keep it going, and to make it happen faster. Of course, there were problems. I was weak, getting sick a lot, and constantly hungry. There were some pressing artistic issues, as well. My piano playing, which wasn't outstanding to begin with, suffered slightly, but the real trouble was with singing. I was in the choir, and it was, by far, my favorite part of camp. We were good, and our choir directors were gentle and brilliant musicians. We sang *Jubilate Deo,* based on the hundredth psalm; a choral suite by Irving Fine based on *Alice in Wonderland*; and a sweet ballad called "Away From the Roll of the Sea" by Allister MacGillivray.

The problem was that I couldn't stand up for extended periods of time without getting light-headed. It became particularly noticeable during rehearsals and longer pieces. We were rehearsing Brahms's *German Requiem*, a fairly long and serious piece, and I kept needing to sit down between movements. One of the other basses in my section kept elbowing me, telling me to get up, but when I'd stand or stay standing for a while, my vision would blur and I'd feel faint. I couldn't really see what was in front of me: it all looked like TV static, then I'd need to sit down. In the last few days of camp, everyone's parents came to see shows and enjoy summertime in the woods. It was time to show them what they'd plunked down all that money for, time to demonstrate what you'd learned. For me, that involved a very lengthy choral concert.

I was standing on the back of the risers, with my fellow basses, when I noticed my eyes were gently drifting into soft focus. I shifted my feet back and forth to snap out of it. I had a drama teacher in junior high who said that people fainted on stage because they locked their knees, so I kept my knees slightly bent and bounced gently up and down. The gnawing in my stomach kept me up for another couple of songs, but eventually the static closed in and light-headedness overwhelmed me. The next thing I remember is sitting on the ground, behind the choral risers. Everyone was still singing. If anyone else in the choir noticed what had happened, they didn't let on. I was blocked by three rows of kids and couldn't be seen from the audience, so I took a moment to get myself together. I got back up and finished the concert. Camp finished, as it had finished every year since 1928, with a performance of Liszt's *Les Préludes*.

M y eating habits remained the same during the beginning of the fall, my sophomore year of high school. I stuck with my crackers-and-oranges diet, sometimes substituting rice cakes for crackers.

I had lost more than thirty pounds during the summer. I wasn't losing weight anymore, though; my diet, meager as it was, kept me hovering around the same weight. No one at school made fun of me for being fat. I saw Jon, my tormenter from world history class the previous year, in the hall during the first couple weeks of school. He looked at me and nodded. "What's up," he said, and kept walking.

But I still had stomach fat, I thought. There was more to do. I began wondering what it would take to keep the weight loss going. I thought that I'd try a couple days of fasting: just drinking water to see where that got me. I tried it one weekday, leaning heavily on the water fountains to get me through nine periods of school, and immediately went home afterward and plopped on the couch in front of the television. Being stationary, I found, kept my mind off of food. I had been drinking a ton of water, though, and had to get up to pee. I stood up, the lights dimmed around me, my vision blurred, the fuzzy static set in, and I was on the floor.

don't remember falling, but I remember waking up and there being blood everywhere. It took me a minute of dazed detective work to figure out that I'd hit my head on an empty green tin of DoubleTree cookies on the floor. There was a cut above my eye, right on my eyebrow line. Nobody else was home, so I stood there in the front hallway for a few minutes and then decided to go outside. Our neighbor, Mr. Lovaas, was across the street doing some yard work. I went up to him and said, "Hi, I just hit my head." He put down what he was doing and looked at me. "Okay, yeah," he said. "You're going to need stitches."

I went to the hospital, but I'm not sure if I called my parents to tell them what happened or if Mr. Lovaas did, or what exactly happened in the days or weeks that immediately followed. The incident turned out to be something of a turning point, although I don't remember any conversations or epiphanies or how exactly my eating habits changed. There were no doctor appointments or psychiatric evaluations—the illness abated as quietly and unacknowledged as it had set in. Statistics about how often eating disorders go away on their own, or with treatment, are imprecise. According to ANRED (Anorexia Nervosa and Related Eating Disorders), people who do not seek professional help for eating disorders may "eventually recover, but it may take several years, even decades." For the "vast majority" of sufferers, it states, it takes three to seven years to recover from an eating disorder. According to Beat, a UK-based eating-disorder charity, 46 percent of anorexia sufferers recover, 33 percent improve, and 20 percent remain chronic sufferers. They also cite "research carried out in Australia" that suggests anorexia lasts eight years, on average. For all of the people who sought treatment for their eating disorders, or were hospitalized, or took part in studies, I imagine there were others, off the record, like me: sufferers who were lucky enough to emerge in a relatively short period of time. Who were fortunate enough not to damage their bodies permanently, or die. People for whom, like my mom said, it was simply a part of growing up.

Joining the JV swim team later that fall really solidified my path toward consuming calories in a healthier, more consistent way. We were a terrible team, horrible athletes individually, and oddballs within the student population. It was the best possible situation. We became each other's support network: we practiced together, burned tons of calories together, and ate together. It was the act of eating with a group of friends that began to normalize food for me. Eating could be something shameful and lonely, certainly—those habits didn't end right away—but it was good to know that eating could also be something that brought you closer to people.

When I was in my bunk at Interlochen, trying to sleep, I'd have recurring fantasies about Thanksgiving stuffing. Thanksgiving is close to my birthday, which is partly why it developed into my favorite holiday, but it's also the fun of everyone coming together over absurd amounts of food. I would lie there, on the top bunk, thinking about stuffing drenched in gravy to block out thoughts of how hungry I was; how I hadn't practiced enough for my lesson the next day; how strange and pointless it felt not to eat when there was so much food available to me; how happy I was to be losing weight and wondering how much weight I had lost; how much I wished I had the body of this older kid who would jog around the athletic field every afternoon; how I dreaded going back to high school but was excited to be in plays in the theater department; girls I liked and thought were cute; when I could get my braces off.

So, at night, when my stomach twisted and growled and disturbed my sleep and I needed to focus on something, I thought about Thanksgiving stuffing. Getting reprimanded for picking off the burned bits of the dark brown crust: the part that had been sticking out the ass of the bird when it was put in the oven. Thinking it was so funny that my mom used the Vincent Price recipe every year, that a creepy old actor had a cookbook. The pliable but slightly firm chunks of bread, tasting of celery, sage, and butter, and moist with turkey fat. Bits of chicken, ham, and giblets bobbing up through a pool of velvety, light brown gravy. My mom, harried but all smiles, unable to sit down until everyone was served and eating. My dad, standing and giving a toast and thanking all of us for coming together to share the meal. **LP**

KOREATOWN

코리아타운

—

Thickeners

How to achieve the
proper level of ooey-gooey
(pg. 118)

PIE V

Recipes

For **SPAGHETTI-AND-MEATBALL PIE** (pg. 108),
BLUEBERRY PIE (pg. 111), and **Liz Prueitt**'s famous
BANANA CREAM PIE (pg. 113)

S PIE

PHOTOGRAPHS BY PETE DEEVAKUL

PIE ROOTS

By Dana Cree

Few parts of my childhood are more valuable to me than the baking education I got from my grandmother. My father's mother, Grandma Eva, was raised in the eastern half of Washington state, the part covered with farms. Her own mother took over as a dairy rancher when her husband opted out of the family, and my grandma was quickly put to work. During her early years, my grandma traveled with her mother, Emma, driving the cows through the Cascade mountains, selling fresh milk to the logging camps. She attended college in the early forties, earning a home-economics degree and discovering an interest in food science in the process.

My first lesson in pie making came when Grandma Eva stayed with us for a week, my parents away on a rare vacation alone. That week was a course in homemaking. She gave me lessons in sewing an apron and a short study in ironing. I remember some pro-tips on making dish washing more enjoyable. It was also time for me to learn how to make pie.

Our neighbors had blueberry bushes that provided the filling. All we needed was a crust. I was just growing taller than Grandma Eva's diminutive stature, and as we stood eye to eye for the first time, she gave me instruction in blending Crisco into flour using a pastry blender. She demonstrated cutting the fat while tossing it with the flour, while a cup filled with ice water was growing colder by her side.

She told me that piecrust was made of small pieces of fat coated in flour, held together with just enough water to moisten them. As she gently tossed the mixture with the ice water, she mentioned to me that some people add vinegar to the pie crust to make it more tender, but she didn't think that was necessary.

She taught me how to squeeze the mixture to check for the correct amount of moisture, and patiently continued adding water, bit by bit, led by confidence and experience. When she pressed the piecrust into two balls, one slightly larger than the other and tucked them into the refrigerator to rest, there was hardly a dusting of flour left on the counter. She made it look easy.

Once it came time to roll the dough, she removed her pie frame from her suitcase (you travel with pie making equipment, no?). It consisted of a dowel-and-wire frame holding a taut square of canvas. Under the patina of flour were three concentric circles: 8, 9, and 10 inches in diameter. She patiently rolled the pie crust (with a rolling pin she also pulled from her suitcase) with even pres-

sure and just a whisper of flour. If one of the edges split, she would put the rolling pin down, dip her finger in ice water, and carefully apply it to the crack. The dough slowly increased in diameter until it fit the assigned circle. She rolled the dough over the rolling pin and carefully unfurled it over the pie pan. A quick tuck, and the crust lined the pan snugly. We filled the shell with blueberries, tossed a little sugar with flour and cinnamon, and sprinkled it over the top. A few dots of butter, and we were ready to roll the top crust and seal our berries.

Grandma Eva taught me to seal the top and bottom together with ice water, before trimming the scraps carefully with a paring knife. We turned and crimped the edges before she cut her signature starburst pattern of pie vents into the top. She added a quick letter "B" in the center of the crust, for Bickford, our family name. We baked our pie at 425 degrees for 15 minutes, to set the crust, and then reduced the heat in the oven to 350. Another 45 minutes or so and we peeked through the vents to see the juices bubbling thick.

I made a lot of haphazard piecrusts after that. I had no patience or finesse, and added much more water than necessary, afraid of my dough cracking on the counter as I whipped the rolling pin back and forth over it eagerly. Martha Stewart inspired my first all-butter crust in college and I cursed the cold butter while doubting the value of the extra trouble as I battled the hard fat. Once the pie was baked, I was shocked by the crisp flaky results and I vowed never to go back to my Crisco roots.

My grandma's pies weren't fancy; she never washed the top for gloss, and she left out as much sugar as she could get away with out of concern for our health. Her simple pattern of vents were functional. Since I started baking professionally, my patience and experience have grown with my exposure to different pies. I use different fats when I make different fillings to achieve nuanced results. I cut an intricate pattern of vents while the top crust is still on the counter, and pinch detailed crimps into the edges. I brush the top with a cream-and-yolk egg wash for maximum shine, and sprinkle it with sugar for a little disco sparkle. My fillings can be untraditional and often include the perfume of a fresh herb or an unexpected spice, and I like to mix three kinds of apples in my apple pie—more if I can get them.

But every pie I make stems from that first lesson, with Crisco, wisdom, and love. To this day I have yet to hear a more thorough explanation of the functional relationship between the ingredients in pie crust. Every time I slide one of my own pies in the oven, I still hope it will live up to Grandma Eva's.

A CRUST FOR EVERY PIE

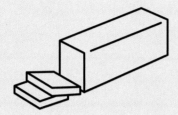

FLAKY ALL-BUTTER CRUST
Best for: Fruit pies

This all-butter crust is the little black dress of my piecrust recipes. It is a versatile, all-purpose crust, but it truly shines as a double-crusted fruit pie. Once in the oven, the butter-rich dough develops flaky layers, which are displayed proudly in the vents cut into the top of the pie. It also works quite well for individually shaped hand pies, or for my favorite pie-making by-product: baked strips of dough sprinkled with cinnamon sugar.

ENRICHED BUTTER CRUST
Best for: Savory pies (see Spaghetti-and-Meatball Pie, pg. 108)

I use this ultrarich piecrust for savory pies. It contains all the wonderful qualities of an all-butter crust, but with the tenderizing addition of more fat. The protein in the egg yolk coagulates when baked, adding a subtle strength to the dough that helps it stand up to the saucy part of savory pies.

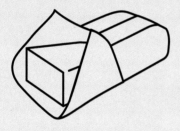

RICH CREAM-CHEESE CRUST
Best for: Decorated pies (see Blueberry Pie, pg. 111)

The cream cheese in this piecrust adds a nice acidity to the dough, which I bolster with a small splash of apple cider vinegar. In addition to boosting flavor, the cream cheese doesn't melt when baked the way butter or lard does, which makes this my go-to crust for decorative tops. Whether it's a carefully woven lattice, a network of overlapping circles individually punched out, or a meticulously pinched rope around the rim, this dough stays put in the oven.

TENDER LARD CRUST
Best for: Blind-baked crusts

Lard is one of the best fats for piecrust, hands down. It's worth seeking out leaf lard—the highest grade of lard, taken from around the kidneys and prized for its softness and flakiness—from your local butcher or farmers' market pork purveyor. Unlike butter, which contains 15–19 percent water, lard is 100 percent fat, meaning the dough doesn't expand as much as a butter crust. This makes lard crust my favorite for blind-baking bottom crusts for pumpkin pie, or for something chilled, like chocolate-cream pie. It stays put when baked, and is fork-tender under delicate fillings.

Flaky All-Butter Crust
MAKES 2 CRUSTS

I only use my hands to make this dough. Pressing the butter into petals makes for a flakier crust than the mechanical pulsing of a food processor or the slicing of a pastry blender. It also allows me to feel the entire process start to finish, picking up subtle nuances in temperature and moisture. If you've never done it, give it a try. It's rare that we have such a hands-on (or hands-in) experience with our food.

275 g	all-purpose flour
4 g	salt
25 g	sugar
225 g	butter, cold, cut into ½" cubes
75–100 g	ice water

1. Combine the flour, salt, and sugar in a large work bowl (about 12 inches in diameter). Transfer the bowl to the freezer for 30 minutes.

2. Once the flour mixture has chilled, remove it from the freezer, and place the butter in the bowl. Working with both hands, begin fishing out and squeezing the cubes of butter into smaller pieces, pressing them into petals and then tossing them back into the flour mixture. Continue until you have flattened them all.

3. Now, use your hands like the upside-down claws of a backhoe: dig each hand into the flour-butter mixture, pulling up a small fistful and letting it rest in the cradle of your curved fingers. Using your thumbs, begin pressing the dough in a rolling motion, moving from your pinkie forward to your index finger. While doing this, let the butter and flour fall from your hands back into the bowl. Continue, occasionally tossing the mixture, until all of the butter pieces are between the size of a grain of rice and a chickpea. Restrain yourself from breaking the butter down too small—the variation in the size of the butter pieces creates the flaky texture of the piecrust when baked.

4. Begin adding the ice water by dripping 2 soupspoons of water over the surface of the butter-flour mixture. Pull the flour mixture from the bottom of the bowl upward, vigorously tossing the entire mixture. Continue, 2 spoonfuls of water at a time, until you have added 75 grams of water and the dough is beginning to form moist clumps.

5. Grab a handful of the dough and squeeze it with about three-quarters of your strength. If it falls apart, add two more additions of water and check again. If it holds together, but falls apart when prodded with your thumb, add 2 more spoonfuls of water and check again. You'll know you have enough water when you can press your fistful of squeezed pie dough and your thumb leaves an imprint, and only a little bit of the dough begins to fall off the sides. It will look just a touch on the dry side, and you might be skeptical that it's actually going to hold together. The flour will continue to soak up the water for the next couple of hours.

6. You will now begin a process the French call *fraisage*. Press the dough with the heel of your hand in a forward motion, compressing the dough and flattening and elongating the butter into flakes. I like to keep the dough in the bowl, as it helps keep all the bits and pieces contained. However, you can turn the mess out onto the counter, which is what you'll see if you Google "fraisage" and obsessively watch videos of people performing this act.

7. Once the dough has come together, divide it into 2 pieces, and shape each piece into a 1-inch-thick disk. The more evenly you press the edges of the disk, the less likely they are to crack and split when you roll your dough. Wrap the disks in plastic wrap and let them rest in your refrigerator for a minimum of 2 hours before you roll your piecrusts. The crusts will keep in your refrigerator for up to 48 hours, and in your freezer for two weeks.

Enriched Butter Crust
MAKES 2 CRUSTS

I prepare this dough entirely in the food processor, which makes it a snap to throw together. Because the liquid is high in fat, there is less risk of tough gluten chains forming under the aggressive agitation of a food-processor blade.

40 g	egg yolks, from 2 large eggs
60 g	heavy cream, cold
275 g	all-purpose flour
4 g	salt
225 g	butter, cold, cut into ½" cubes

1. Place the egg yolks and cream in a small bowl and whisk until combined. Hold in the refrigerator until ready to use.

2. Place the flour and salt in a bowl and toss to combine. Transfer the bowl to the freezer for 30 minutes.

3. Once the flour mixture has chilled, remove it from the freezer, and transfer it to the bowl of a food processor along with the butter. Pulse the food processor 10 times. Now, a pulse is not a nervous jump in which you release the button as quickly as you press it. A pulse is an intentional motion, lasting about 1 second. If you were waltzing with your food processor, you would hold the pulse button for the 1 and 2 counts, releasing it on 3. After 10 pulses, the butter should be broken down into nuggets ranging in size from Nerds to M&M'S. Remove the lid from the food processor and drizzle the reserved egg-cream mixture over the surface. Pulse the food processor a few more times, until the dough begins to clump together. Pulse one more time to pull the moist clumps into a large mass.

4. Turn the dough out onto a lightly floured surface and continue to use your hands to press the dough together. Divide it into 2 pieces, and shape each piece into a 1-inch-thick disk. The more evenly you press the edges of the disk, the less likely they are to crack and split when you roll your dough. Wrap the disks in plastic wrap and let them rest in your refrigerator for a minimum of 2 hours before you roll your piecrusts. The crusts will keep in your refrigerator for up to 48 hours, and in your freezer for 2 weeks.

Rich Cream-Cheese Crust

MAKES 2 CRUSTS

I use a food processor to cut the fat into the flour, breaking up the cream cheese first, then the butter second. The cream cheese becomes smaller than the butter, which keeps the dough from changing shape when baked. However, I don't use the food processor to add the liquid, instead turning the flour and fat out into a bowl and sprinkling the liquid in bit by bit. I find that a food processor can be overly aggressive, forming too many gluten chains once liquid is added. This recipe is sized slightly larger than most other double-crust recipes to give you a little extra dough to cut and shape for decorations.

350 g	all-purpose flour
5 g	salt
25 g	sugar
150 g	cream cheese
150 g	butter, cold, cut in ½" cubes
25 g	apple cider vinegar, chilled
100–125 g	ice water

1. Place the flour, salt, and sugar in a bowl and stir until evenly combined. Cut the cream cheese into ½-inch pieces, and toss them with the flour. Place the bowl in your freezer for 30 minutes.

2. After 30 minutes, remove the bowl from the freezer and transfer the flour and cream cheese to the bowl of a food processor. Pulse the food processor 8 times. A pulse is not a nervous jump in which you release the pulse button as quickly as you press it. A pulse is an intentional motion, lasting about 1 second. If you were waltzing with your food processor, you would hold the pulse button for the 1 and 2 counts, releasing it on 3. After 8 pulses, add the butter. Pulse an additional 8–10 times until the butter is broken down into nuggets ranging in size from Nerds to M&M'S.

3. Turn the mixture out into a large work bowl (12 inches in diameter). Begin adding the vinegar and ice water by dripping two soupspoons of liquid over the surface of the butter-flour mixture. Pull the flour mixture from the bottom of the bowl upward, vigorously tossing the entire mixture. Continue, two spoonfuls of water at a time, until you have added 75 grams of water and it is beginning to form moist clumps.

4. Grab a handful of the dough and squeeze it with about three-quarters of your strength. If it falls apart, add two more additions of water and check again. If it holds together, but falls apart when prodded with your thumb, add 2 more spoonfuls of water and check again. You'll know you have enough water when you can press your fistful of squeezed pie dough and your thumb leaves an imprint, and only a little bit of the dough begins to fall off the sides. It will look just a touch on the dry side, and you might be skeptical that it's actually going to hold together. The flour will continue to soak up the water for the next couple of hours.

5. You will now begin a process the French call *fraisage*. Press the dough with the heel of your hand in a forward motion, compressing the dough and flattening and elongating the butter into flakes. I like to keep the dough in the bowl, as it helps keep all the bits and pieces contained. However, you can turn the mess out onto the counter, which is what you'll see if you Google "fraisage" and obsessively watch videos of people performing this act.

6. Once the dough has come together, divide it into 2 pieces, one a little larger than the other, with the intention of the larger piece being rolled for the decorative top crust. Shape each piece into a 1-inch-thick disk. The more evenly you press the edges of the disk, the less likely they are to crack and split when you roll your dough. Wrap the disks in plastic wrap and let them rest in your refrigerator for a minimum of 2 hours before you roll your piecrusts. The crusts will keep in your refrigerator for up to 48 hours, and in your freezer for 2 weeks.

Tender Lard Crust

MAKES 2 CRUSTS

If you are vegan, this is the piecrust for you—simply swap out the lard for vegetable shortening, which will behave in the same manner. If you store your shortening in the cupboard, chill it before you proceed.

275 g	all-purpose flour
4 g	salt
25 g	sugar
200 g	lard, straight from the refrigerator
75–100 g	ice water

1. Place the flour, salt, and sugar in a large work bowl (12 inches in diameter). Cut the lard into 1-inch pieces, and add them to the bowl with the flour. Begin cutting the fat into the flour by pressing the tines of a pastry blender into the fat, then tapping the pieces off back into the flour. Continue pressing the pastry blender into the large chunks of lard until they are all broken down.

2. Now you can use the round edges of the bowl and the round tines of the pastry blender collaboratively. Begin cutting the fat into the flour by rocking your wrist in a swiping-cutting motion around the sides of the bowl. Pause to tap out any fat that is building up between the tines from the pastry blender, and toss the mixture with your hands to encourage even distribution. Continue cutting the lard into the flour until you have a very crumbly mixture made of very small pieces of fat. The mixture will resemble couscous.

3. Begin adding the ice water by dripping two soupspoons of water over the surface of the lard-flour mixture. Pull the flour mixture from the bottom of the bowl upward, vigorously tossing the entire mixture. Continue, two spoonfuls of water at a time, until you have added 75 grams of water and it is beginning to form moist clumps.

4. Grab a handful of the dough and squeeze it with about ¾ of your strength. If it falls apart, add two more additions of water and check again. If it holds together, but falls apart prodded with your thumb, add 2 more spoonfuls of water and check again. You'll know you have enough water when you can press your fistful of squeezed pie dough and your thumb leaves an imprint, and only a little bit of the dough begins to fall off the sides. It will look just a touch on the dry side, and you might be skeptical that it's actually going to hold together. The flour will continue to soak up the water for the next couple of hours.

5. Once your dough holds together when squeezed, divide it into two pieces, and shape each piece into a 1-inch-thick disk. The more evenly you press the edges of the disk, the less likely they are to crack and split when you roll your dough. Wrap the disks in plastic wrap and let them rest in your refrigerator for a minimum of 2 hours before you roll your piecrusts. The crusts will keep in your refrigerator for up to 48 hours, and in your freezer for 2 weeks.

Rolling Dough, Step by Step

For any of the preceding crust recipes:

1. Remove a disk of pie dough from the refrigerator. Before you unwrap it, knead it a little with your hands, pressing it down against the counter with the palm of your hand. The tension of the plastic wrap will help keep the disk shape as you work the dough to become less brittle and more malleable.

2. Unwrap the dough and lay it on a lightly floured surface. Begin rolling the dough out with slow, even pressure. Dust with flour as necessary, and flip the dough over every few rolls. This ensures your dough isn't sticking to the counter, and puts even pressure on both sides of the dough as they grow, preventing large splits.

3. If the dough splits on the edge, pause and brush any flour off of the edges of the crack, then moisten your finger with water and press both sides of the split together with your fingers to mend the tear. Dust the area lightly with flour, then flip the pie dough over and do the same to the other side. Continue rolling, taking special care not to apply too much pressure to that area.

4. Roll the piecrust out until it is about 2 inches wider in diameter than your pie plate. Place the rolling pin at the bottom of the pie dough and roll toward the top, folding the pie dough over the rolling pin so it curls around the pin like a scroll.

5. Carefully unfurl the piecrust over your pie plate, adjusting as necessary so it is centered. Press it gently until it takes the form of the pie pan. It should hang over the edges by about an inch.

SPAGHETTI-AND-MEATBALL PIE

MAKES ONE 9-INCH PIE

This savory filling is the perfect match for the Enriched Butter Crust recipe. I made this pie for family meal while helping my friend Jason Stratton open the aperitif bar Artusi in Seattle. The staff consumed copious amounts of pasta, eating the remnants of precise shapes and the dried strings of tajarin left over from the night before. In an effort to keep it interesting, I came up with spaghetti-and-meatball pie. Once the words spaghetti pie got stuck in my head, I became obsessed. What resulted is exactly what it sounds like. We used leftovers, much like I imagine you might, but I wouldn't hold myself back from boiling pasta and rolling meatballs solely for the purpose of making this pie. I'll leave it to you to find a recipe for spaghetti sauce and meatballs.

600 g	cooked spaghetti
500 g	spaghetti sauce
50 g	chopped parsley
150 g	parmesan, grated fine
300 g	heavy cream
2	Enriched Butter Crusts
9	meatballs, each about the size of a golf ball

1. Heat the oven to 425°F.

2. Place the cooked spaghetti, spaghetti sauce, and chopped parsley in a medium-sized bowl and toss until even. Set aside.

3. Sprinkle the parmesan in an even layer on a baking sheet lined with a Silpat. Place the baking sheet in the oven and roast the cheese for 5 minutes, until it is a little oily, golden brown, and nutty smelling. Remove the pan from the oven and transfer it to a wire rack to cool.

4. Once cool, transfer the roasted parmesan to the jar of a blender. Place the cream in a small pot over medium-high heat. Cook the cream until it comes to a full, rolling boil, then pour it into the blender jar with the roasted parmesan. With the blender on high, purée until velvety smooth, about 2 minutes. Transfer the parmesan cream to a bowl, and set aside at room temperature.

5. Roll out 1 disk of Enriched Butter Crust according to the instructions on page 107.

6. Place the spaghetti in the pie shell. Place one of the meatballs in the center of the pie, then spread the rest around the perimeter, about an inch away from the edge. Drizzle the parmesan cream over the top so that it covers the spaghetti evenly. Set aside while you prepare the top crust.

7. Roll out the second Enriched Butter Crust to a diameter 2 inches larger than your pie plate.

8. Brush the lip of the bottom piecrust with water, then unfurl the top piecrust over the spaghetti, matching the edges with the bottom crust. Use your fingers to press the top and bottom crusts together, then use a pair of scissors to neatly trim away the rough edges, leaving ½ inch of crust hanging over the edge. Tuck the edge under itself, so the seam is turned in, and press the lip to lock in all the juices. Crimp the edges in any decorative style you wish, then cut a small, 2-inch X in the center of the pie. Fold back each resulting flap of dough, dab it with water, and secure it to the top crust, leaving a small empty square vent in the center of the pie.

9. Bake the pie for 15 minutes, then reduce the heat to 350°F. Bake for another 30–45 minutes, until the crust is golden brown. Remove and let rest for 15 minutes before slicing.

BLUEBERRY PIE

MAKES ONE 9-INCH PIE

This juicy filling is well suited to the Rich Cream-Cheese Crust, which stays in place once cut decoratively and adds a pleasant richness. I'm giving you instructions for a classic lattice top, something all pie bakers chase to perfection.

1 kg blueberries
(or substitute huckleberries, double the sugar, and omit the lemon juice)
100 g sugar
15 g cornstarch
1 lemon, zested and juiced
5 g cinnamon
2 Rich Cream-Cheese Crusts
50 g butter
+ 9" circle of clean cardboard

Egg Wash
1 egg yolk, whisked together with 50 g milk or cream

1. Heat the oven to 350°F.

2. Place the blueberries in a large bowl. Add the sugar, cornstarch, lemon zest and juice, and cinnamon, and toss until the berries are evenly coated. Set aside.

3. Roll out 1 disk of Cream-Cheese Crust according to the instructions on page 107.

4. Place the blueberry mixture in the pie shell, spreading it evenly into a nice mound. Cut the butter into ½-inch pieces and dot the surface of the filling evenly.

5. Roll out the second cream-cheese crust to a diameter of 11–12 inches. Slice the crust in half, then into ¾-inch strips, working from the center out toward the edges. You want to have 14 strips in total.

6. Set the cardboard circle on the counter and dust it lightly with flour. Place one of the longest strips down the center of the circle. Lay shorter strips about 1 inch from either side of the center strip. Continue using strips of descending length until you have reached the edges of the circle and used up half of the pie strips. They will look like the bars of a jail cell.

7. Take the bottom edge of the center strip and fold it upward over itself, so the edge in your hand is just a little longer, overlapping the top edge. Leave the 2 strips on either side of the center, and take the next 2 strips and fold them up over themselves as well. Leave the last 2 unfolded.

8. Now, lay the longest strip of remaining dough down the horizontal center of the circle, over the still-extended strips. Dab a little water on the places where the pieces will intersect. Press lightly against the dough where it crosses. Unfold the other strips of dough, again dabbing a little water where they cross with the horizontal one.

9. Take the strips you left unfolded last time and fold them up from the bottom, stopping where they cross the horizontal strip. Lay the next-longest remaining strip about 1 inch below the center horizontal strip. Dab the vertical strips with water where they intersect and press lightly. Unfold the folded strips, and secure the intersections with a dab of water. You will notice a basket-weave pattern emerging.

10. Continue this process, folding alternating strips up to make room for a new horizontal strip, then switching for the next addition, leaving 1 inch between each strip. Repeat for the top half of the circle. You will end up with a proper lattice top made of crosshatched strips of pie dough, with 1-inch empty squares between them.

11. Brush the surface of the lattice top with the egg wash while it is still on the cardboard, then brush the exposed lip of the pie bottom. Lift your cardboard over the center of the pie, about an inch or two above the pie. Carefully shimmy the cardboard out from underneath the lattice, tipping it slightly so the dough slides off over the center of the pie. Adjust so it is centered.

12. Press the edges of the lattice against the lip of the bottom crust, and use scissors to trim the rough edges, leaving ½ inch of overhang. Fold the overhanging bottom crust over the lattice edges, creating a 1-inch lip around the edge of the pie. Use your fingers to press a decorative edge into the lip, sealing the edges of the lattice tightly. Egg-wash the sealed edge.

13. Bake the pie for 45 minutes to 1 hour, until the juices from the berries bubble thick and the lattice top is golden brown. Allow the pie to cool completely so the juices have a chance to thicken; if you cut it before the juices set, they will run out. Warm pie is a true delight, and if you wish to eat it this way, warm a piece back up.

111

A HISTORY OF THE WORLD'S BEST BANANA CREAM PIE

By Liz Prueitt

My first forays into making cream pies would have been when I was really little. Kids love the texture and familiarity of it—it's just like pudding. When I was growing up, my dad would always make tapioca pudding, and we would make all sorts of cream pies, the vanilla wafer–style cream pie, and those icebox cakes with whipped cream and chocolate cookies. All those kid kinds of things.

The banana cream pie was the first cream pie that we made at Tartine, and without even realizing it, I probably used the cream pies we made growing up as a point of reference. My father loves bananas and cream pies. Now when my family comes to visit we have to have it in the refrigerator. If I haven't brought one home, my parents will stop at the bakery on the way to the airport and have one.

When I was coming up with the recipe, I thought about somebody who might take it home and not eat it until the next day, or who might want leftovers after that. The first thing we always consider is how to make the pastry so that it keeps in a sort-of-perfect state. You want to be able to control the quality of the pie as best you can three days after it's left the bakery.

You have to think about each component and decide if it's going to be purely functional or part of the flavor. With a cream pie, you think, *How do I deal with a really wet filling and a crispy crust?* That's what led us to coating the shell with chocolate. In this case, the chocolate works so well—it's both functional and a flavor in the pie. There are other ways of sealing a crust, but none of them are going to be as good as painting it with a chocolate barrier.

The filling we use is not a thick custard—it's set with cornstarch, which I tend to favor over flour. I don't like a super-thick flour-set custard, because it feels so industrial. All those industrial pies use flour, which gets gummy too easily. Ours is definitely a little more fluid than most, but that doesn't really bother me. We also use a ton of vanilla. I think that's where people go wrong with cream pies: not adding good flavoring. Salt and acid start making it actually taste like something. It's not like a crème brûlée, where you have a thin layer of thick custard topped with the nice caramelized sugar to break through the richness. You need to have a balance of richness and sweetness in your cream pie.

Under the custard, we layer caramel because it just goes so well and it's kind of nice to have a little surprise in the pie. I love cutting into a pie and having this gooey caramel on the bottom. (Technically, we bake our banana cream pie in a straight-sided tart shell, but it's as deep as pie. I just like the tart form more than the pie form.)

When we first put the Tartine menu together, we wanted to include everything that we love. And since we were making all these components for the banana cream pie, we also decided to make a coconut cream pie. When you're in production for a bakery or a restaurant, you want to be able to utilize your ingredients in more than one way. We use the same pastry-cream base for the coconut cream pie and also for the éclairs. You can do the same at home.

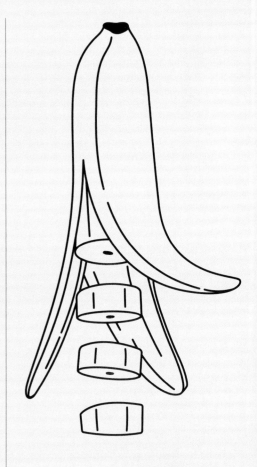

Banana Cream Pie with Caramel and Chocolate

MAKES ONE 10-INCH PIE

1	10" pie shell, baked and cooled
3 oz (85 g)	bittersweet chocolate, coarsely chopped
1 C (250 ml)	very cold heavy cream
2 T (30 ml)	sugar
⅓ C (75 ml)	Caramel
2½ C (625 ml)	cold Pastry Cream
2	ripe bananas, sliced into ¼"-thick rounds
3 oz (85 g)	bittersweet chocolate bar for making curls (large bars are best), at room temperature

1. Have the pie shell ready for filling. Fill a saucepan with about 2 inches of water, set it over medium heat, and bring to a simmer. Place a stainless-steel bowl over (but not touching) the water. Put the chopped chocolate into the bowl and heat, stirring occasionally with a rubber spatula, just until the chocolate melts and is smooth. Remove from heat.

2. Using an offset spatula, dry pastry brush, or the back of a spoon, spread the melted chocolate evenly over the bottom of the pie shell. Refrigerate for 10 minutes to set the chocolate.

3. Meanwhile, pour the heavy cream into a mixing bowl or stand mixer fitted with the whisk attachment. Whip the cream until slightly thickened, then add the sugar and continue to whip to medium-firm peaks.

4. Remove the pie shell from the refrigerator and drizzle the caramel evenly over the chocolate. Scoop the pastry cream into the shell. Arrange the banana slices evenly over the pastry cream, and then lightly press them into the cream. Using an offset or rubber spatula, spread the reserved whipped cream on top.

5. Rub the smooth side of the chocolate with your palm to warm it slightly. Using long strokes, scrape the surface of the chocolate with a chef's knife to form curls. Scatter the curls over the top of the pie.

6. Chill the pie until the pastry cream is set, at least 3 hours. Serve the pie cool. It will keep in the refrigerator for up to 4 days.

Caramel

MAKES ABOUT 1½ CUPS

⅔ C (150 ml)	heavy cream
¼	vanilla bean
1¼ C (240 g)	sugar
¼ C (60 ml)	water
¼ t (1 ml)	salt
2 T (30 ml)	light corn syrup
¾ t (4 ml)	lemon juice
4 T (55 g)	unsalted butter, cut into 1" chunks

1. Pour the cream into a small, heavy saucepan. Split the vanilla bean in half lengthwise and use the tip of a sharp knife to scrape the seeds from the pod halves into the milk. Place the pan over medium-high heat and bring to just under a boil, stirring occasionally. Reduce the heat to low to keep the cream warm.

2. In a medium, heavy saucepan, combine the sugar, water, salt, and corn syrup. Bring to a boil over medium heat, stirring to dissolve the sugar. Then cook, without stirring, until the mixture is amber colored, 5–8 minutes.

3. Remove the caramel from the heat. Carefully and slowly add the cream to the sugar syrup. The mixture will boil vigorously at first. Let the mixture calm down, then whisk until smooth. Add the lemon juice. Let cool for about 10 minutes.

4. Add the butter to the caramel one piece at a time, whisking after each addition. Whisk the caramel periodically as it continues to cool. The caramel will keep in an airtight container in the refrigerator for up to 1 month.

Pastry Cream

MAKES 2½ CUPS

2 C (500 ml)	whole milk
½	vanilla bean
¼ t (1 ml)	salt
4 T (60 ml)	cornstarch
½ C + 1 T (4 oz)	sugar
2	large eggs
4 T (55 g)	unsalted butter, cut into 1" pieces

1. Have a bowl ready with a fine-mesh sieve resting in the rim. Pour the milk into a heavy, nonreactive saucepan. Split the vanilla bean in half lengthwise and use the tip of a sharp knife to scrape the seeds from the pod halves into the milk. Add the salt, place over medium-high heat, and bring to just under a boil, stirring occasionally to make sure that the milk solids are not sticking to the bottom of the pan and burning. There's no rescuing burnt milk.

2. Meanwhile, in a nonreactive mixing bowl, whisk together the cornstarch and sugar. Add the eggs and whisk until smooth.

3. When the milk is ready, slowly ladle about one-third of the hot milk into the egg mixture, whisking constantly. Pour the egg-milk mixture back into the hot milk and continue whisking over medium heat until the custard is as thick as lightly whipped cream, about 2 minutes. In order for the cornstarch to cook and thicken fully, the mixture must come just to the boiling point. You want to see a few slow bubbles. However, if the cream is allowed to boil vigorously, you will curdle the pastry cream. Remove from heat and immediately pour through the sieve into the bowl. Let cool for 10 minutes, stirring occasionally to release the heat and prevent a skin from forming on top.

4. When the pastry cream is ready (it should be about 140°F), whisk the butter into the pastry cream 1 tablespoon at a time, whisking until smooth before adding the next tablespoon.

5. Cover the bowl with plastic wrap, pressing the wrap directly onto the top of the cream, and chill. Be careful whisking the cream once it is cold—overmixing will break down the starch and thin the cream. Pastry cream will keep, well covered, in the refrigerator for up to 5 days.

A TIME FOR TOPPINGS

By Emily Elsen, Four & Twenty Blackbirds

There are times when a double crust will not do—in fruit season, for instance, when I'm in heaven because of the abundance of fresh-fruit pies with crumble or streusel on top.

Streusel and crumble are defined differently in different regions of the United States—but when it comes to pie in our kitchen, our crumble is made with oats, butter, brown sugar, white sugar, and spices. The oats make it really dense and toothy, almost like an oatmeal cookie or a granola. Our diners actually refer to it as "the pie with the granola on top," but it's not *quite* granola, because it's *filled* with butter. Our streusel is really simple: just butter, flour, and white and brown sugars. To us, streusel is what you put on top of a coffee cake. It's light and sweet, and really nice when it gets a little brown and there's a toastiness to it.

We've probably tried a crumble or streusel on every single flavor pie that we make at some point. We do a plum crumble and call it "plumble pie" and it's really delicious, but plum streusel is also delicious. A really delicate sour cherry balances well with a little streusel on top, which doesn't overwhelm the cherries.

When it comes to the best application for each, moisture, sweetness, and density are key. For example, rhubarb and crumble are excellent together because rhubarb is substantial and holds up to the heavier, more flavorful topping. Our cranberry-and-sage pie, which we've traditionally made with a lattice top, is also delicious as a crumble pie. Blueberry-streusel is great, because streusel is lighter and crisps up and lets some of the moisture in the berries come out. We've had experiences where somebody's a little heavy-handed with the crumble on a blueberry pie, and all of the crumble sinks to the bottom and the blueberry squishes and bubbles over, and then you end up with a crumble pie with blueberry sauce. It isn't any less delicious, but it's not what we're going for.

Oat Crumble Topping & Crust

MAKES 2 CUPS, ENOUGH FOR ONE
9-INCH PIE TOPPING OR CRUST

2 T	granulated sugar
¼ C	packed light brown sugar
¾ C	rolled oats
⅓ C	all-purpose flour
½ t	kosher salt
⅛ t	ground allspice
⅛ t	ground cardamom
⅛ t	ground cinnamon
4 T (½ stick)	unsalted butter, cut into ½" cubes, at room temperature

1. In a large bowl, stir together all of the ingredients except the butter. Sprinkle in the butter pieces and toss to coat, then rub the butter into the dry ingredients with your fingertips until the butter is incorporated and the mixture is chunky but not homogeneous.

2a. If using for a crumble top, chill for at least 15 minutes before using.

2b. If using for a crust, press the mixture evenly into the bottom and up the sides of an ungreased metal 9-inch pie pan. Freeze until solid, about 15 minutes. Meanwhile, heat the oven to 350°F. Bake on the middle oven rack for 18–20 minutes. If the crust slumps or cracks while baking, gently push the crumble back into place with a clean, folded kitchen towel while it's still hot. Cool completely before filling. The crust will keep refrigerated for 5 days or frozen for 1 month.

Streusel Topping

MAKES 1½ CUPS, ENOUGH FOR ONE
9- OR 10-INCH PIE TOPPING

1 C	all-purpose flour
3 T	packed light brown sugar
4 t	granulated sugar
1¼ t	kosher salt
6 T	unsalted butter, cut into ½" cubes, at room temperature

Stir together the flour, brown and granulated sugars, and salt in a large bowl. Sprinkle in the butter pieces and toss to coat. Rub the butter into the dry ingredients with your fingertips until the butter is incorporated and the mixture is chunky but not homogeneous. Chill for at least 15 minutes before using. The streusel will keep refrigerated for 5 days or frozen for 1 month.

A SIMPLE EQUATION FOR ICE CREAM PIE

In my house, pie tins are only used for ice cream pies, because they take literally ten minutes to throw together and, on the axis of deliciousness, they are pretty damn close to the top. All you have to do is 1) take a mallet to a bag of cookies, toss the crumbs with melted butter, and press the mix into a pie tin, then 2) fill the "crust" with store-bought ice cream that you've let sit out for a few minutes to soften. Pop it back in the freezer, and it'll keep as long as you need it to, which makes ice cream pie the ideal pie for entertaining.

Theoretically, any cookie and any ice cream can be combined to make a pie. You could smash a bunch of Thin Mints and cram some mango sorbet into the crust, but I can't recommend that. On the next page is a table of cookie and ice cream possibilities that all but the worst grocery stores should have on hand, and how I would recommend combining, and, if you're really going for gold, top them. Consult it, add to it, amend it, make it yours. **—BRETTE WARSHAW**

THE EQUATION

$$\frac{(\text{8 ounces crushed-up COOKIES} + 6\tfrac{1}{2} \text{ tablespoons melted BUTTER}) \times \text{1 pint ICE CREAM}}{} $$

= **THE BEST PIE**

	OREOS	CHOCOLATE CHIP COOKIES	GRAHAM CRACKERS	CHOCOLATE WAFERS	ANIMAL CRACKERS	NILLA WAFERS	SHORTBREAD	GINGERSNAPS
VANILLA	Drizzle with fudge sauce	Top with chocolate shavings	Top with toasted walnuts	Drizzle with fudge sauce	Top with rainbow sprinkles	Top with more crushed Nilla Wafers	Top with toasted slivered almonds	Drizzle with honey
CHOCOLATE	Top with chocolate shavings	Top with whipped cream	Top with mini marshmallows (optional: toast with a torch)	Top with crushed pretzels	Drizzle with condensed milk	✕	Serve with scotch	✕
MINT CHIP	Top with whipped cream	Top with chocolate shavings	✕	Drizzle with fudge sauce	✕	✕	✕	✕
COFFEE	Top with chocolate shavings	Drizzle with fudge sauce	Top with granola	Top with more crushed chocolate wafers	Drizzle with caramel	Top with more crushed Nilla Wafers	Drizzle with caramel	⚠
COOKIES AND CREAM	Top with whole Oreos	Top with chocolate shavings	⚠	Top with more crushed chocolate wafers	Pointless, avoid	✕	✕	✕
STRAWBERRY	Top with whole Oreos	What are you, seven?	Top with halved strawberries	Drizzle with fudge sauce	Top with whipped cream	Drizzle with caramel	Top with halved strawberries	⚠
COOKIE DOUGH	Top with chocolate shavings	Top with more crushed chocolate chip cookies	Pointless, avoid	Drizzle with fudge sauce	⚠	✕	✕	✕
PISTACHIO	✕	✕	Top with whipped cream	✕	Arrange a zoo of animal crackers on top	Top with toasted pistachios	Top with more crushed shortbread	Top with toasted pistachios

⚠ = **THIS IS PROBABLY GROSS, PROCEED WITH CAUTION**   ✕ = **GOD FORBIDS IT**

THICKEN IT

How many times has your beautifully flaky and crisp piecrust gotten soggy because you didn't properly tend to your fruits and let their juices run out like teenagers in the night? It's time to reel in that water, activate that pectin, and slice a clean piece of pie.

The innate thickener in all fruits is pectin, a carbohydrate in plant cell walls that releases at high heat. Boiling fruit with sugar causes pectin molecules to hold on to each other as they disperse throughout the filling. While at a boil, the chains of pectin get tangled up with the sugar that's suspended in the fruit's water molecules. The molecules chill out as the filling cools after baking, and as they settle, water gets trapped inside the pectin, forming a gel and yielding a perfectly set filling.

Pectin content varies by fruit and is most plentiful in a plant just before it's fully ripe. And even when their pectin content is high, not all fruits have enough to produce a beautifully set filling. This is where thickeners come in. Starch thickeners absorb water molecules and restrict water movement as they grow, helping to form a fruity gel or thicken a custard.

—ARALYN BEAUMONT

CORNSTARCH: Cornstarch is super fine and contains no protein, so it disperses and absorbs water without restriction. It's a strong binding agent and activates at boiling temperature. Its downsides are that acids tend to break down its starch molecules, it's not completely flavorless, and it can produce a cloudy color, so it's best in a well-seasoned custard pie.

FLOUR: This is your grandma's favorite thickener, but maybe it's best left in her pantry. Because of its high protein content, it has a weaker concentration of starch (75 percent), which increases the risk of clumping while the rest of the filling stays runny. It's suitable for sturdy fruits like apples that require a long baking time.

GELATIN: Gelatin is a product of heated collagen, which is found in animal skin, connective tissue, and bone. It's a long, thin structure that is really attractive to water, and when the two combine, they settle into an elastic structure that can readily support air bubbles—ideal for chiffons and mousses. Gelatin sheets and powder have to be activated (bloomed) in water before being added to a filling.

TUBER STARCHES (TAPIOCA, POTATO, ARROWROOT): These starches contain no protein, so they're effective even at low concentrations. They activate at low temperatures, yield a silky texture, and have no flavor. They're ideal for light and watery fruits like berries. They are much more delicate than other starches so treat them with respect (refrain from overstirring and overheating). Dotting the filling with small pieces of butter can help prevent boiling and thus keep your delicate starches from breaking.

MISCELLANEOUS: Apples have so much pectin that grating them into your berry pies gives a boost to whatever thickening agent you're using.

HELPFUL TIPS FOR THICKENING

FRUITS WITH HIGH PECTIN CONTENT include apples, cranberries, gooseberries, plums, and grapes. Keep in mind that pectin content will vary by species.

FRUITS WITH LOW PECTIN CONTENT include apricots, blackberries, blueberries, cherries, peaches, pears, raspberries, and strawberries.

FOR FRUIT PIES, macerate the fruit for an hour to release some of the juices. Discard excess juice and mix the fruit with thickener and spices.

MIX THE THICKENER with whatever dry ingredients you're adding to the filling. This way the flavoring and thickening agents will disperse throughout the entire pie, leaving no clumps or bland spots behind.

THE TIGHTER YOU PACK THE FRUIT, the less room for the juices to travel and the tighter your filling will set.

SMALLER PIECES OF FRUIT cook more quickly, which is good for delicate starches.

DOESN'T THIS LOOK SO YUMMY?

Doesn't this look so yummy? Isn't it so clever? Why restrict your pie to insipid vanilla ice cream? You can put *anything* on pie! Think of all the possibilities this simple idea opens up: rocky road on apple, cherry on pecan, praline on cherry, salted caramel on blueberry, lemon sorbet on chicken pot pie.

Now stop. That's gross.

The truth is that vanilla* is the only ice cream you should be setting atop a warm slice of pie. Anything else is like wearing a baseball cap with a suit. You think it's cool, but it really just looks like amateur hour. Only Ron Howard can pull it off. Are you Ron Howard? I didn't think so.

—CHRIS YING

---

* And a couple close cousins. Crème fraîche, maybe.

CACIO E PEPE

Mazzo	No. 9 Park	Momofuku Noodle Bar
MARCO BACCANELLI	BARBARA LYNCH	TONY KIM

Photographs By Gabriele Stabile

Pasta with cheese: preferred sustenance of children everywhere, bane of their precocious friends and ambitious parents.

Enter cacio e pepe, which, technically, is pasta with cheese, but also much more. It's one of the classic pasta dishes of Rome, one that Marco Baccanelli—a Roman chef whose recipe you'll find on the next page—describes as "violent." And he's right: the sharpness of pecorino Romano cheese and heat of fresh black pepper whacks what would be a comfortingly bland bowl of food into one that is genuinely exciting to eat—and to cook. (Coaxing finely grated cheese and water together is more fun than, say, dumping a cup of parmesan onto egg noodles.) The result is mac and cheese that you can serve to adults and feel sophisticated and worldly about and think, *Oh, look at this great technique I have*. It's a bowl of pasta and cheese that both my current and child selves—really, anyone—can get behind. Here are three takes on it: the aforementioned from Baccanelli of Mazzo in Rome; a playful one from Barbara Lynch of Boston restaurants Menton, No. 9 Park, Sportello, and many others; and a vaguely Asian one from Tony Kim of Momofuku Noodle Bar. —Brette Warshaw

121

MARCO
BACCANELLI

I was born in Rome and grew up in the Centocelle neighborhood. I could tell you, as a Roman, I'm from here—Roman culinary tradition is my mother tongue. *But really, I think that's bullshit.* Cucina romana: *sure, everybody does it here, but who does it well? Your birth certificate by itself doesn't count for shit—you still need perfect execution and technique. For example, I believe that the Japanese are the best in the world at making cappuccinos—their technique is spotless! Pizza is another thing like that. It's not just good in Naples—there's awesome pizza around the world, too.*

Our approach to Roman food comes from studying it. We're not from the ranks of those chefs who can do every technical thing but don't know anything about tradition. We love Roman tradition, we respect it deeply, and we study it constantly. The research never stops.

Cacio e pepe, as the tradition goes, seems like the simplest thing ever: pasta, pecorino, and pepper. The dish was born in the pastures of Lazio; in the winter, shepherds would eat slices of homemade pasta dough (water, flour, and salt) with pecorino and black pepper—the pepper would keep them warm. Our approach is to tweak the traditional recipe here and there—with respect, without changing the game—but with a more thoughtful approach. Instead of hot water, we add pepper broth to the cheese, which enhances the lighter, more delicate qualities of the *pepper. We still grind pepper on the dish before serving so you have that stinging flavor, but by using the infusion beforehand we have better control over two aspects of the same ingredient.*

When cooking this dish, it's fundamental to let the pepper broth cool down a little before mixing it with the cheese. It should not be higher than 130 degrees. If the water is too hot, the cheese will start to coagulate and the fat will separate, creating gummy lumps on one side and watery casein on the other. You don't want that. Every pecorino has a different fat mass and will react differently when

mixed with the warm water, so test it first. (This time around, we used Brunelli pecorino Romano.) When the pasta is finished cooking, let it cool for thirty seconds to a minute before mixing it with the broth-cheese emulsion, to avoid the same problem.

In Rome, most people just bring drained pasta and cheese and pepper out into the dining room, and mix it at the table. Or, worse—so cliché—they'll mix it in the shell of a pecorino wheel. That, for us, is unacceptable. This is a fast, furious, violent dish, and it's the technique and the tradition that make it so delicious.

CACIO E PEPE

MAKES 1 SERVING (CAN BE MULTIPLIED, BUT EACH SERVING MUST BE ASSEMBLED SEPARATELY)

80g	semolina flour, plus more as needed
20g	00 flour, plus more as needed
+	kosher salt
1	large egg
½ t (1 g)	crushed black peppercorns
40 g	finely grated D.O.P. pecorino Romano cheese, plus more for garnish
+	freshly ground black pepper

1. Blend the semolina flour, 00 flour, and a pinch of salt in a wide bowl and create a well in the center. Crack the egg into a small bowl set on a scale. If the egg does not measure 50 grams, top it off with a few drops of water until it reaches the correct weight. Beat the egg with a fork or whisk, then pour it into the well. Work the flour into the egg, bit by bit, bringing flour into the egg from the edges of the well. Once you have a loose, shaggy dough, set the fork aside and begin kneading the dough in the bowl. When you have a cohesive mass, turn the dough out onto a lightly floured surface and knead it until it is smooth and does not crack or fray when gently stretched, about 8–10 minutes. Wrap the dough in plastic wrap and let rest at room temperature for 1 hour, or in the refrigerator overnight.

2. Unwrap the dough and divide it into 3 pieces. Use a rolling pin to form each into an oval thin enough to be fed through the thickest setting of your pasta machine. Pass each piece of dough through the thickest setting several times, folding the dough in thirds and rotating it with each pass, until you have a uniform rectangle that is about 10 inches long and ⅛-inch thick. (If you need to move to a thinner setting to achieve this, feel free.) Dust the dough with semolina and let rest and dry for 10 minutes.

3. Affix the spaghetti attachment to your dough roller. (We're actually making *tonnarelli*, not spaghetti, since the resulting noodle will be square at the end, not round.) Once the pasta sheets are leathery to the touch, pass them through the cutter. Gather the tonnarelli and dust them lightly again with semolina. Arrange on a rimmed baking sheet in a loose single layer, and cover with plastic wrap. Refrigerate until ready to cook, up to 2 days. (The noodles will be notably more springy and delicious after 1 day of rest in the fridge.)

4. When you're ready to cook, bring a large pot of salted water to a boil over high heat. Meanwhile, combine the crushed peppercorns with 3 tablespoons water in a small saucepan and bring to a simmer. Cook for 2 minutes, then remove from the heat; it should have reduced by about half. Let steep until ready to use.

5. Drop the tonnarelli in the boiling water and set a timer for 5 minutes.

6. When assembling the cacio e pepe, timing and heat are important. Place the grated cheese in a bowl. Pour the warm pepper broth over the cheese, leaving most of the peppercorns behind. Use a rubber spatula to mash the cheese and pepper broth together until you have a granular paste. Drizzle a spoonful or two of slightly cooled pasta water over the cheese, continuing to stir and mash and drizzle until you have a sauce the consistency of béchamel. Keep the sauce warm, but not over direct heat. When the timer goes off, check the pasta. Once it's al dente, drain it into a colander, reserving ¼ cup pasta water. Toss the pasta a couple of times to release some heat, and let it stand for 1 minute to cool slightly. (If the pasta is too hot when added to the cheese, the cheese will congeal into unappetizing lumps.) Add the tonnarelli to the pecorino sauce and toss, adding splashes of pasta water to create a creamy emulsion that clings to the noodles. Transfer the pasta to a warmed bowl and top with a sprinkle of pecorino and a few grinds of pepper.

Translated by Gabriele Stabile

BARBARA LYNCH

The first time I went to Italy, I was twenty-one, and it was my first time outside the States. It was really my first time out of South Boston, where I grew up. I went with my friend Sarah Jenkins to her family's house in a little town called Teverina, about an hour-and-a-half north of Rome, and it was the best trip ever. She taught me how to make gnocchi; we'd go shopping at the market; there was a huge prosciutto in the middle of the kitchen table. I've loved Italy ever since.

Anellini look like little Cheerios—I actually ate them for breakfast the other day. The shape is traditionally used for vegetable sauces or brothy sauces made with thick chicken stock. It can be cooked in a sauce for longer than other shapes and stay chewy. This gives you a bigger window of time when making something like cacio e pepe, since you don't have to worry as much about overcooking your pasta while you're trying to get the water and cheese to behave together.

Some tips: Before you start cooking your pasta, make sure all of your ingredients are ready to go. Incorporate the pasta water and cheese in stages, so that they better coat the pasta. Some people use a mix of parmesan and pecorino, but I think pecorino melts better. Garnish it all with frico—crisp cheese wafers—for texture, and you've got yourself a great bowl of Cheerios.

ANELLINI ALLA PECORARA

MAKES 4 SERVINGS

+	kosher salt
+	**Anellini**
5 T + 1 t	unsalted butter
1 C	grated pecorino
+	**Frico**, for garnish
+	freshly ground black peper

1. Bring a large pot of salted water to a boil over high heat. Drop in the pasta and cook until the pieces float to the top, about 5 minutes. Drain, reserving some of the cooking water.

2. Place a large saucepan over high heat. Add 1 tablespoon water, and gradually whisk in the butter until melted. Add the drained pasta and a few dribbles of the cooking water, and toss until combined. Add around half of the pecorino, and toss again. You want the cheese-butter mixture to coat the pasta; if it needs more liquid, use more pasta water. Add another ¼ cup pecorino, and toss until melted.

3. Divide the mixture into shallow bowls and garnish with the remaining pecorino. Break up the frico on top of each bowl and grind a few turns of black pepper on top. Serve immediately.

ANELLINI

1 C	all-purpose flour
1 C	semolina flour
1 T	freshly ground black pepper
1 t	kosher salt
1 t	baking powder
½ C	warm water, plus more as needed

1. In the bowl of a stand mixer fitted with a hook attachment, combine the all-purpose flour, semolina, pepper, salt, and baking powder. With the motor running, drizzle in the water, letting the dough come together after each addition. If the dough is too dry, add more water 1 tablespoon at a time. Mix until the dough is smooth and firm, about 4 minutes. Let rest for about 15 minutes under a slightly damp towel.

2. When you're ready to roll out the dough, pull off a small palmful, keeping the rest covered until needed. Break off a pea-sized piece, roll it into a thin string, and press the ends closed, forming a Cheerio-like shape. Repeat for the remaining dough, working with small hunks at a time. Set the anellini aside.

FRICO

1 C	grated pecorino

Place a nonstick sauté pan over medium heat. Add a few mounds of cheese, and cook until the cheese melts and begins to crisp, about 3 minutes. It should be a light gold color. Flip and cook the other side until crisp, about 2–3 minutes more. Cool on paper towels. Repeat with any remaining cheese. Set the frico aside until ready to use.

TONY KIM

Conventionally, cacio e pepe is made with water, pecorino Romano, and black pepper. That's all there is. It's the texture of the sauce that everyone is going for—this creamy mixture that just kind of glazes the pasta. It's a perfect example of what cooks like to make for themselves: something simple that still takes some kind of skill to get right.

My idea with this version was not necessarily to improve or complicate cacio e pepe, but to do my own take on it. I took away the cheese component and replaced it with butter mixed with a little chickpea hozon, which is like miso made with chickpeas instead of soybeans. Instead of using just black peppercorns, I added Sichuan and white peppercorns, so there was a little more variety in the heat. And then I used fresh ramen noodles in place of spaghetti or bucatini—I like something with a little more chew.

Even though we're using Japanese ramen, we're still going to use some Italian sensibilities. We're going to cook our noodles very al dente, so that they have the texture and chew we want, and finish them in the sauce. That way, the sauce gets absorbed into the noodles a little bit, and the starch helps bring the whole dish together. With a conventional cacio e pepe, you'll see a lot of vigorous stirring happening during this stage, trying to get the cheese and water and starch to emulsify. Here, we have the hozon to help the sauce bind. The emulsification process pretty much happens on its own.

This is a great thing to make for yourself, but you can scale it up, too. The whole process only takes around four minutes, start to finish. It's not meant to be overly contrived—it's a really fun, simple thing to cook, and I think it does the true Roman cacio e pepe justice. Not bad for a Korean kid in New York, right?

"CACIO" E PEPE

MAKES 1 SERVING

+	kosher salt
1 T + 1 t	butter, softened
2 t	chickpea hozon or white miso
½ C	chicken stock, plus more as needed
1 t	freshly ground Sichuan pepper, plus more for garnish
1 t	freshly ground white pepper, plus more for garnish
1 t	freshly ground black pepper, plus more for garnish
1 portion	fresh ramen noodles

1. Bring a pot of salted water to a boil over high heat. Meanwhile, in a small bowl, mix together the butter and hozon until smooth.

2. Melt the hozon butter in a large saucepan over medium heat. Add the chicken stock, Sichuan pepper, white pepper, and black pepper, and bring the mixture to a boil.

3. Drop the noodles into the boiling pot of water and cook until they are relaxed but firmer than al dente, about 1–2 minutes. Using chopsticks or tongs, lift the noodles out of the water and into the hozon-butter mixture. Stir and toss the noodles in the sauce until cooked through, about 1–2 more minutes, adding a little bit more chicken stock if the sauce seems too thick. The noodles should be lightly coated in a peppery sheen. Add a pinch of salt, toss one more time, and heap onto a plate.

Sprinkle lightly with each of the peppers, and serve.

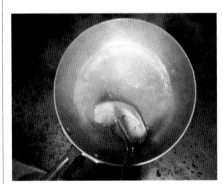

127

BARBARIAN DAYS

Surfers—the obsessive, up-before-dawn types that lurk quietly among us, secretly wiping away drips of seawater from their noses at their desks—will tell you that surfing is not a sport. And they're correct in that. Besides the professional tour (which bears even less resemblance to nonprofessional surfing than professional basketball does to a game of H-O-R-S-E), surfing is not a competition between people.

You might jockey for position and curse novices ("groms"), but no, in surfing, your conflict is not with your fellow man. It is with the infinite natural variables—amplitude, period, angle, wind, time, the shape of the ocean floor—that mean the difference between a perfect, rideable wave and a crushing, foamy death trap. Surfing is a perpetual fight to commune with nature, to force two immiscible bodies, you and the ocean, to cooperate.

It's not an easy pursuit to explain or make interesting to non-surfers. I worried about this when I started reading William Finnegan's surfing memoir, *Barbarian Days*. I like Finnegan a lot. I love his writing for the *New Yorker,* and

I was pulling for him in the way that one pulls for other surfers on good days when there are plenty of waves to go around: you *woot!* for them when they make a wave, and I wanted him to make this one.

So it was wonderful to find in *Barbarian Days* a captivating and sympathetic story about a decades-long case of wanderlust that had Finnegan chasing waves and stories from Los Angeles to the South Pacific, Southeast Asia, South Africa, the Gold Coast of Australia, and Portugal. I was also struck by the frequency of passages about food.

Barbarian Days is not a food book, but it adeptly demonstrates food's ability to communicate a sense of place and time. In other words, I think you can read and enjoy these excerpted food scenes without any idea of what is going on in the story. You can feel the youthful urgency with which a teenage Finnegan sucks on discarded mango rinds as he rushes desperately to get to the beach. You can see him grow from a *haole* kid naively snacking on uncooked sausages, to a husband and father sharing parrot fish with his wife when the surf is bad.

—Chris Ying

ONE
OFF DIAMOND HEAD
Honolulu, 1966–67

There was strange fruit—mangoes, papayas, lychees, star fruit—that my mother learned to judge for ripeness, then proudly peel and slice.

On special occasions we went to a restaurant called the Jolly Roger, part of a pirate-themed chain, with burgers named after Robert Louis Stevenson characters, in a shopping mall in Kahala.

My father's work carried us into odd orbits. A hyperkinetic restaurateur named Chester Lau, for instance, had attached himself to Hawaii Calls, and for years my family turned up at far-flung luaus and pig roasts and civic events organized by Chester and usually held at one of his joints.

The islands were blessed with a large food surplus; their inhabitants were not only skilled fishermen, terrace farmers, and hunters, but built and managed elaborate systems of fishponds. Their winter harvest festival lasted three months—during which the surf frequently pumped and work was officially forbidden.

We each got a heavy sack of Portuguese sausage and basic instruction in door-to-door salesmanship. We were raising money for our surfing club—a wholesome cause, like the Boy Scouts... A couple of haole ladies took pity on me, but I made few sales. The day got hotter. I drank from yard hoses, but I had brought no food. Finally, famished, I tore into one of my sausages. It wasn't tasty, but it was better than nothing. Ten minutes later I was on my knees, retching into a storm drain. I didn't know that Portuguese sausage had to be cooked. I wondered, between heaves, if I was getting closer to or farther from the glory of surf-club membership.

Roddy and I would sneak into the gardens and lobbies of the neighboring hotels, and while one of us stood lookout, the other would dive in and plunder fountains and wishing wells for coins. Then we'd go buy *chow fun*, *malasadas* (Portuguese doughnuts), and pineapple slices from a street cart.

There was a diner on the pier. My family ate there on beach weekends. From our booth by the window, I could see surfers out at a spot known as California Street. They were silhouettes, backlit by low sun, and they danced silently through the glare, their boards like big dark blades, slashing and gliding, swift beneath their feet. California Street was a long cobblestone point, and to me, at ten, the waves that broke along its shelf seemed like they were arriving from some celestial workshop,

their glowing hooks and tapering shoulders carved by ocean angels. I wanted to be out there, learning to dance on water. The snug fracas of the family dinner felt vestigial. Even my chiliburger, a special treat, lost its fascination.

TWO
SMELL THE OCEAN
California, ca. 1956–65

The Beckets' house overflowed with full-time residents, and yet it somehow doubled as a community center. There were always neighbors in and out, platters of tacos arriving from the kitchen, someone barbecuing fresh-caught fish in the backyard, live lobsters going in the pot. Among the adults, the wine and beer and liquor flowed.

When a passenger ship known as the Great White Steamer came in from the mainland, local kids would swim out to it and shout for the tourists on deck to throw coins. I was probably eight or nine and I joined them, chasing the dimes and nickels that fell near me, twisting and flashing into the turquoise depths. We stored in our cheeks the coins we snatched as we shouted and battled for more. I remember swimming back to my family's boat and spitting my haul into my hands in the cockpit. I had enough for a corn dog on shore, maybe even one for Kevin.

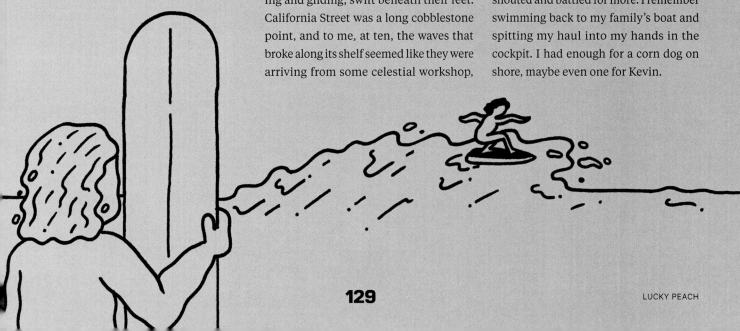

THREE
THE SHOCK OF THE NEW
California, 1968

Domenic's grandparents had made a barnful of wine from a vineyard that no longer existed, and it was all turning to vinegar in blue plastic Purex jugs in the barn behind Domenic's house. We took to helping ourselves to a jug on weekend nights, drinking it slug for gasping slug in the dark on the edge of a storm culvert behind the barn. The warm valley night would turn woozy, hilarious. I loved Domenic's imitations of his addled, good-hearted grandpa, whose favorite exclamation was, for some reason, "Murphy, Murphy, Murphy!" I once tried to make my own contribution to our drinking cache by raiding my parents' liquor cabinet, pouring half an inch from each bottle into a milk carton. Never mind that I was mixing bourbon with crème de menthe with gin—the tiny individual thefts would never be noticed. And they weren't. But Domenic and I got sick as dogs from the concoction. Only the loose supervision at his house let us get away with our heaving and hangovers.

FOUR
'SCUSE ME WHILE I KISS THE SKY
Maui, 1971

We were eighteen. It was springtime. We were camping on a headland at the west end of Maui, sleeping in a grassy basin under an outcrop of lava rocks. A little pandanus grove helped block the view of our campsite from the pineapple fields up on the terrace. This was private property, and we didn't want the farmworkers to spot us. We were raiding their fields at night, trying to find ripe fruit they had missed. We always seemed to be camping on somebody else's property in those days.

When the school year ended, we pooled our savings, quit our gas station jobs, said good-bye (I assume) to our parents, and set off, zigzagging east, in Domenic's van. We were sixteen, and we didn't even take our boards.

We got as far south as Mazatlán, as far east as Cape Cod. We dropped acid in New York City. We subsisted on Cream of Wheat, cooked on a Coleman camping stove.

But Domenic, taking a piss at first light, saw the surf. "William! We got waves." He called me William only on serious occasions, or as part of a joke. This was a serious occasion. We had run out of food the night before, and had been planning a run to Lahaina, the nearest town, which was twelve miles away, for provisions. That plan was postponed indefinitely. We scavenged for nutrients—gnawing old mango rinds, scraping out soup cans, choking down bread previously rejected as moldy.

We grabbed our boards and jogged around the point, screaming "Fuck!" and hooting nervously at each gray set that passed the headland, darkening on the final turn into the bay.

We found secluded coves where we could build campfires, and beaches with water as clear as gin. I showed Caryn how to find ripe mangoes, guavas, papayas, wild avocados.

Everybody at Kobatake's got food stamps. Indeed, everybody who had ever lived there seemed to have gotten them. "At the usual time of the month, the pink came," was how Caryn's ever-mordant journal put it. She meant the dozens of pink government checks that arrived for residents both current and departed. This mass reliance on food stamps carried, among our loose group of peers on Maui, no particular assumptions, I thought, about the welfare state.

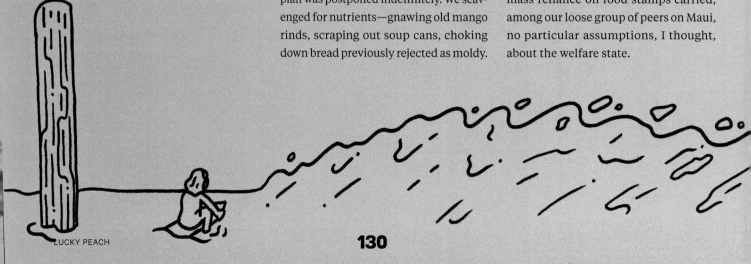

THE SEARCH
The South Pacific, 1978

Speaking of anthropology, I found on Pohnpei a collision of local tradition with modernity—and this would turn out to be an inescapable theme everywhere in the Pacific—over how to get drunk. In the evenings the men either drank, in a slow, ceremonial, communal ritual, using coconut shells as cups, a mild indigenous liquor called *sakau*—it's called other names on other islands, most commonly kava—or else they drank imported alcohol. Imported alcohol, whether spirits or beer, cost money and was associated with colonialism, fighting, bars, general dissipation, and I hung with the sakau crowd, on principle, even though I found the stuff, which was viscous and gray-pink and medicinal-smelling, vile. It numbed the mouth, though, and after eight or ten cups it tilted my brain to an angle from which I began to understand, or believe I understood, a complex form of checkers that was the local pastime.

On our last night in Sala'ilua, Sina gave us a feast. We had been eating well all week—fresh fish, chicken, coconut crab, clams, papaya soup, yams, and a dozen variations on taro (with spinach, with banana, with coconut cream). Now came pork sausage and banana bread with icing, somehow prepared over an open fire. Also a sharp-tasting black-and-green delicacy from the sea bottom—I missed the name—that toyed embarrassingly with my gag reflex.

Bryan and I had learned not to show up in remote villages empty-handed. Ballpoint pens and balloons for the kids were optional, but something for the chief or the coastal landowners really wasn't. The best gift, the traditional offering, was an armload of the root from which kava is made. In Fiji it's called *waka*. We had planned, leaving Suva, to buy a batch at a farmers' market near the bus station, but suddenly our early-morning bus was leaving and, in haste, we dodged into a shop and bought a fifth of Frigate Overproof Rum instead. The rum would be welcome, we figured, and we were right. The problem was that when we reached Nukui, a village near the bay we wanted to check—this was after a long ride in an outboard-powered canoe through a maze of impressively dense mangrove swamps—the headman, Timoci, who greeted us warmly, insisted on opening the rum immediately and passing the flagon around the small circle of men who happened to be on hand. We polished off the bottle in fifteen minutes. It was still early afternoon. We were now kneewalking. We never made it to the beach that day.

They showed us where wild papaya trees grew, not too far into the bush, and where good eating fish tended to run near shore at high tide. The tide was coming in now, and would soon be full enough, I thought, to let them cross the reef, but Bob said the wind was blowing too hard. They would spend the night. He would light one of the signal fires later to let their families in Nabila know they were here. Peter took a handline to the fishing spot and quickly caught a string of a dozen gray mullet. We grilled them on sticks, ate with our fingers, and washed the meal down with green coconut milk. Bob inspected our supplies. He was not impressed with our unused fishing gear. He ordered Peter to leave us some stouter line and better hooks. High above us, the wind thrashed in the coconut trees. The sun dropped into the western Mamanucas.

Our fishing was pitiful. Even with the hooks and line the guys had left, and knowing the best spot and tide, we couldn't seem to catch a thing. I pried an octopus off the reef, pounded and boiled it to a fare-thee-well, using way too much freshwater, and it was still too tough to eat. (I should have used salt, I learned later. That was if we had salt.) We did a piss-poor job generally of living off the land and sea. We soon picked and ate all the ripe papayas we could find. I climbed the shortest, most wind-bent palm trees for green coconuts, but I was defeated by the taller, straighter trees. There were lots of beefy bats with yellow-striped faces—they hung like gray seedpods in the upper story of the jungle by day and swooped overhead at night—that would probably have made great fruit-bat soup. We had no notion of how to catch them. There were crabs of various types, but the ones that looked like the best eating lost their allure when we saw how efficiently they excavated and devoured human excrement.

SIX
THE LUCKY COUNTRY
Australia, 1978–79

In a big restaurant kitchen, we were at the bottom of the job ladder, below the dishwashers, who were all women. We peeled potatoes (which we called Idahoes), handled the garbage, did the nastiest scrubbing, and hosed down the greasy floors with hot water at the end of the night. And yet we made an excellent wage (I could save more than half my earnings) and, as employees, we had entrée to the casino's private members' bar, which was on the top floor of the building. We would troop up there after work, tired and ripe, and throw back pints among what passed for high rollers on the Gold Coast. Once or twice, my coworkers spotted the owner of the casino in there. They called him a rich bastard and he, properly chagrined to be rich, bought the next shout.

Distances between outback towns are sometimes measured in "tinnies"—how many cans of beer it takes to traverse them. It was at least a dozen tinnies to the main road north, also dirt, which we met in a village called Kingoonya, where a tumble-down roadhouse offered the world's most welcome steak burgers, served by Australia's most beautiful waitress.

SEVEN
CHOOSING ETHIOPIA
Asia, Africa, 1979–81

We stayed in a cheap, clean *losmen* (guesthouse) in Kuta Beach, ate well for practically nothing, and surfed daily. I found a good writing spot in a college library in Denpasar, the provincial capital, catching a bus there each morning. It was a cool, quiet refuge on a hot, noisy island. My novel was rocking along. A street vendor with a little turquoise cart would show up outside the library at midday, my signal to knock off. He served rice, soup, sweets, and *satay* through the opened windows of campus offices. I liked his *nasi goreng*—fried rice.

I had vowed to be more careful about what I ate and drank after my Bali paratyphoid follies. I was still eating at street stalls, though, and we were still staying in dives.

I started a list of things I wished we'd brought: honey, whiskey, duct tape, dried fruit, nuts, powdered milk, oatmeal. More protein would be welcome. Meat and even, oddly enough, fresh fish were rarities in Lagundri. Our meals were mostly rice and collard greens, with hot chilies to help fight bacteria. Like everyone, we ate with our hands. A fisherman in Java had taught me the best way to eat rice with your fingers. You used the first three fingers as a trough and the back of the thumb as a shovel. It worked. But I needed more food, more vitamins. My boardshorts were falling off my hips.

I had been felled briefly in Singapore by another fever, which a doctor had said was malaria. It must have been a mild case, I figured, when the symptoms passed. Sharon urged me to eat more rice and noodles. I was all ropy muscle. A body needed some fat reserves. And it was lovely, I realized, to have somebody looking after me, looking *at* me, like that.

We rented a little house in the jungle in southwest Sri Lanka, paying twenty-nine dollars a month... We had no electricity and drew our water from a well. Monkeys stole unguarded fruit. Sharon learned to make delectable curry from our landlady, Chandima.

My own classroom, New Room 16, had been taken over by a group of senior girls who had prepared a banquet. There was a huge pot of curry, and a great array of Cape Malay specialties: *bredie, samoosas, sosaties, frikkadels,* yellow rice with raisins and cinnamon, roast chicken, *bobotie, buriyani.* School had let out by then, and the other teachers were invited. June Charles, my youngest colleague—she was only eighteen yet teaching high school—guided my father through the strange and tasty dishes.

EIGHT
AGAINST DERELICTION
San Francisco, 1983–86

The surf was fierce but mediocre; there was no one else out. The smell of fresh doughnuts drifted across the water from a bakery near Wise's shop.

NINE
BASSO PROFUNDO
Madeira, 1994–2003

Madeira was a shock to the senses— sheer green coasts, tiny cliff-hugging roads, Portuguese peasants studying our boards suspiciously, waves surging heavily out of deep ocean. We drove through gorges and forests, over high, vertiginous ridges. We ate *prego no pão* (a garlic steak sandwich) at roadside cafés and tossed back espressos.

Most of the Portuguese immigrants to Hawaii had come, it seemed, from Madeira. The malasadas (Portuguese doughnuts) we ate as kids had come from here, as had the Portuguese sausage that I once wolfed down uncooked.

I came to a little café. I had been there before, and the owner gave me coffee and a bun on credit. From the raised café steps, I could see the ocean. Great sets were now reeling down the coast, even bigger than earlier. The rip channel had vanished. So I had caught a brief window of big, highly concentrated, well-organized waves at a spot that was no longer there. My luck had been extravagant. I felt like finding a church, lighting a candle, and humbling myself.

What was I doing? Why was I here? I was a grown-up, a husband, a citizen, full of conventional public-spiritedness in my real life. My American life. I was forty-four years old, for Christ's sake. And not a churchgoer. Everything felt unreal, including my sense of disbelief. And yet the cup in my hand did not shake. Indeed, the weak instant coffee tasted sublime.

She made the most of the perks: the obscure, often raggedly beautiful spots I dragged her to; the freedom to read; the seafood. For an inlander, she had a remarkable affinity for shellfish. In Madeira, she favored the *espada* at the Tar Mar and the young wine known as *vinho verde*.

Even if we didn't find waves, Caroline and I had found a café in the north that served a grilled parrot fish that justified any expedition.

TEN
THE MOUNTAINS FALL INTO THE HEART OF THE SEA
New York City, 2002–2015

We could talk waves until any non-surfers in earshot, starting with our wives, fled in horror. We did it on surf runs, over surf mags and videos, at sidewalk cafés on Broadway, trading shots of tequila, which Selya called "loudmouth soup."

It had been a sweet week. Nosing up the Chesapeake, we put into hamlets you would never find by road. We ate hard crabs, soft crabs, blue crabs, she crabs. Shot the breeze with waitresses and tackle shop owners. My father and I had always shared an affection, bordering on compulsion, for checking out obscure places. 🄻🄿

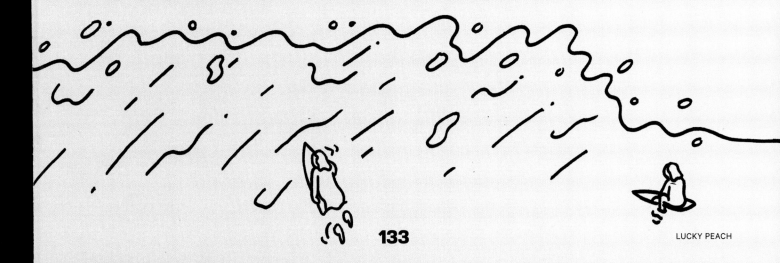

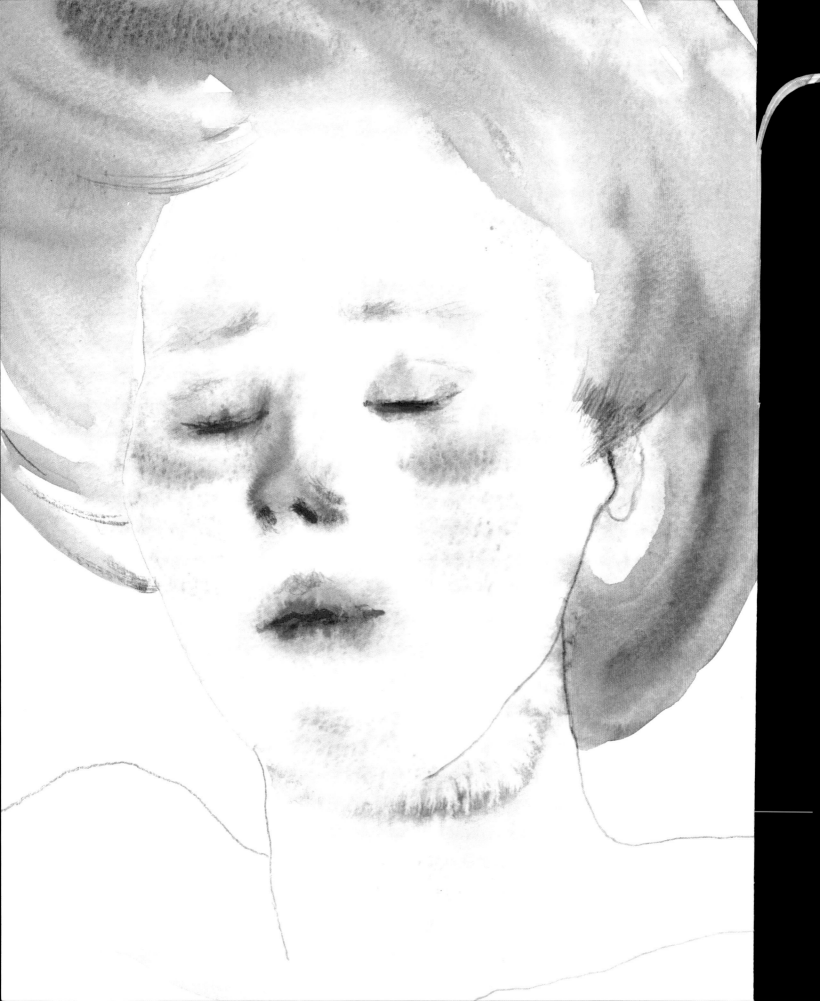

OIL & VINEGAR

Fiction by Amelia Gray

Illustrations by Alice Moloney

Lissa began to so look forward to her bath that she took one every night. She would drop her tote bag at the door and pull off her clothes before she got to her pantry, where she poured herself the first of two glasses of wine.

She kept the oil by the bath because she never cooked in the first place—the whole nightly bath idea started simply because she was about to throw the oil out with the idea of off-loading the things that didn't bring her joy. Standing with the oil in one hand and the trash bag in the other, she decided to give it a shot.

A few drops in the bath, the magazines advised in articles about soothing rituals using items from around the house. She considered making a facial mask with baking soda and lemon before discovering the lemons hard as stones, their seeds rattling inside. So she took the olive oil to the bathroom and added five careful drops to the water. They floated on the surface like pearls. Churning the water up, she found the drops split and shrank, gathering around her ankles when she stepped in.

It was a luxurious experience for Lissa, who had long insisted on the benefits of a good shower, the feeling of it all vanishing down the drain. In fact she had never taken a bath, though she always pretended she had when conversations turned toward the activity and others spoke of waterlogged books and candles and precariously balanced glasses of wine. It all sounded too affected to her, and though she told herself she was a practical woman and not given to the overly precious, once she tried it, she was hooked. She started to skip her quick morning shower and distracted herself at work by scrolling through images of bathtubs. She gathered books and a proper loofah and one of those wooden panels that stretched from one side of the tub to the other and could hold a few tea lights and a glass of wine. And though her routine evolved, the olive oil component remained the same. She liked the scent, which reminded her of sitting in the kitchen with her grandmother.

Though it was enough for months to add a few drops to the water, Lissa soon discovered that a more generous pour markedly improved the benefit. While with a few drops she noticed softer skin, a quarter cup healed the calloused ridges on her feet and cured her lower back of the raw skin where her jeans rubbed her waist. The first time was a pure accident. Upending the bottle left her hair as nourished as an oil slick, and the oil sank into her pores. And though cleanup required a full hour spent scrubbing the bathtub with endless paper towels and chemicals that burned her hands, her oil bath had become as natural to her routine as a daily vitamin.

She confided in her work friend one morning, gloating a little in the way you do when, without really trying, you have improved your own life.

"Do you mix the oil in?" Susan asked.

"I kind of stir it around with my hands."

"It sounds weird." She was skeptical but had begun taking notes on the back of a case file regarding the quantity and brand of oil and the methods Lissa used. "I have a rash," she said. "Do you think it would help?"

"I bet it would."

"Doesn't it clog the tub?"

It did, a little. Lissa had noticed the water draining more slowly. Little flies buzzed across the surface of the standing water.

Susan flipped open the file, uncapping her highlighter. "I'm trying apple cider vinegar next," she said. "A shot of it in the morning and at night helps with skin conditions and cellulite. I'm stocking up. It doesn't make sense to do something unless you do it all the way."

That night, Lissa poured the last of the bottle into her bath and opened another. Susan's words echoed in her ears: *Skin conditions and cellulite. Do it all the way.* She opened a gallon jug of oil and poured it in at once, slipping in after. The oil rested atop the water like a slug on a cake, but she thrashed her arms a little and it mixed to change the color of the water to a weak greenish hue, like a peridot. She floated in the oil and imagined herself as a seal pup. There was a glorious weightless feeling, and when she was full of wine, she felt like the main course of the most intimate Italian family dinner, candles winking on the linen.

She left the tub to drain, but when she got up the next morning, the water was still standing. When she called the landlord, she couldn't bear to tell him the truth about her mistake, and so she lied and said that a rowdy child under her care had upended the pantry into the tub. (After that, he was certain she was operating an illegal day care on the premises and set up a security camera to watch the comings and goings of her front door.)

"That's where you messed up," Susan said over sandwiches. "Never blame children. It comes back to you eventually."

"You're right." Lissa did feel very intensely that she had messed up. Her whole body had a tendency to turn a plummy shade when she was embarrassed, which was easily and often.

She wondered whether the oil might help ease these sudden bouts of anxiety. "How was your bath last night?"

"Best thing I ever did. I'm totally exfoliated, internally and externally. My toxins have split completely, my hair is free of impurities. I'm five pounds lighter." Her skin did seem radiant, as if she had taken it off and scrubbed it in the sink before sewing it back on tighter around the edges. "The trick is to not dilute it at all," she said. "I used forty gallons. It stung for the first few minutes, but I could feel it healing me. Actually I care less about slights and problems in my day-to-day." To demonstrate, she picked up a thick case file she had brought to lunch and threw it in the trash. "I don't care," she said.

Lissa stopped at the warehouse store and bought jugs of oil in bulk, loading her hatchback until it sagged on its axles. She considered the price difference between olive oil and canola, the devastating effect the splurge would have on her weekly budget, but she had so many problems that this one item could solve: hair loss, cellulite, skin elasticity, acne, scars. Mild to moderate depression. A lack of interest in painting for going on five years now. On the way out of the store, she saw a sixty-gallon cooler and went back in to place it on hold. She would have to make two trips.

At home she took a hot shower and then sat in the cooler and poured the oil in around her. She felt like a chicken breast in a marinade. Her only purpose in that moment was to accept the oil into her pores. She was buoyed by the oil and contained within it. She stayed like that for one hour and then two. Once or twice she held her breath and went under completely.

When she emerged unsteadily, reaching to the wall for support, she found her hands were plump and poreless, slick with nourishment. Her eyelashes were dark and full, her hair glistened with new life. Best of all, the cooler didn't need to be emptied right away. It had a spout for when the oil needed to be changed, and wheels, which meant she could drag it outside to drain off the porch. Lissa pictured the oil brimming with toxins, hued a rusty black, like what drained from her car.

"A cooler is a fantastic idea," Susan said. They were eating chicken breasts from the cafeteria. Susan had five chicken breasts lined up on her plate and ate them methodically, reserving the edges like crusts from a sandwich. Her skin had the raw shine of a scrubbed baby. "Now you can take it anywhere."

Lissa piled her chicken breasts in the center of her plate, drowning them in barbecue sauce. "You should get one," she said.

"My bathtub is so clean, though."

"Yes, but where is that dirt and soap scum and everything from the bathtub going? Probably right into your skin."

Susan frowned. "There's no way to know," she said.

"Get a cooler and come to my house. We can set them up on the patio."

This was the first time Lissa had invited a coworker into her home. She worried for a second that she had messed up, that her new friend would never speak to her again and she would go back to spending these long lunch hours in front of her computer. But Susan shrugged like it happened every day. "Sure," she said.

As Lissa prepared her home for a visitor that evening, she thought about how simple friendship was and how much easier it made every aspect of her life. She placed books on different tables in case Susan wanted to pick one up and thumb through it. She filled a cereal bowl with candy but, finding it strange, poured the candy back into its bag and filled the bowl with almonds instead.

Susan arrived, dragging a cooler up the driveway. Lissa had spent some time maneuvering her own onto the back patio, where a line of cypress trees kept the neighbors from seeing, and unlocked the gate to the backyard. Susan dragged the cooler through the dirt and arranged it next to Lissa's so that the plastic hatches opened to face each other.

"Wine?" Lissa offered.

"Too many tannins," Susan said, going back to her car for the vinegar.

Lissa blushed hard and took the bottle back inside. It was possible she was taking in far too many tannins. She poured it down the sink.

When she came back out, she found Susan pouring the last jug of apple cider vinegar into her cooler. She stripped down methodically, folding clothes and placing them on a deck chair before she stepped in, hugging her knees to her chest as she sank down into the fluid. She shivered with a slight chill. With the vinegar up to her chin, she inhaled and coughed a little. The vinegar's acid was tickling her nose. "It's nice," she said.

Lissa removed her clothes as well. She had brought a bath-ing suit but stuffed it under her jeans, not wanting to make her guest feel uncomfortable. The oil would have been significantly warmer than the vinegar, and though she had used it the night before, it still looked pure and clean. Though she realized too late that she had neglected to shower, she didn't feel the usual feelings of embarrassment for forgetting. The oil filled the empty spots around her body.

She stretched a little, enjoying the familiar feeling. Glancing over at Susan, she noticed the other woman was gazing blankly at the cypress trees on the property line. "They can't see us," Lissa said.

"Could you close my lid?"

"To your cooler?" Lissa felt confused, and then stupid, because Susan couldn't possibly have meant any other lid, despite the fact that closing it with her inside didn't make any sense. Perhaps she didn't mean she would be inside. "With you inside?" she asked, feeling immediately stupid for that question also. Of course she meant for it to be closed with her inside, or else she would close it herself.

"And lock it," Susan said.

"Why would you want that?" Stupid, stupid question. Susan had her own reasons and they were perfectly admirable, Lissa was certain. Every thought she had humiliated her. The oil slipped around her and she felt certain that she would somehow slip out of the cooler and tumble down the stairs into the dirt.

Susan was certainly looking at her like she was stupid. "I'm over it," she said.

"Of course." She still didn't understand, but it was as good an answer as any. "Goodbye," she said. Lissa braced herself against Susan's cooler to reach the lid as her friend sank deeper in the vinegar, deep enough that only the two tips of her nostrils remained above the liquid. Before they went under, she could have sworn Susan rolled her eyes.

Lissa closed the latch on Susan's cooler. There was a muted sloshing sound, and then it was quiet. She felt very alone on the porch and very cold. She let the oil rise up over her chin and lips, and reached behind her head to pull the plastic strap connected to her lid. It tipped gracefully forward and tapped her on the head, going down with her as she sank into darkness. She heard it seal.

The white walls of the cooler had become the boundary of her entire world. There was no sound she didn't create herself, no sensation that did not begin and end in her own body. She closed her eyes and tried to will her heart to stop. **LP**

COOK LIFE

DUCK TALE

ILLUSTRATED BY BRECHT VANDENBROUCKE

The first episode of Cook Life comes from a Bangkok-born chef, who moved to the States and quickly made friends with other recent immigrants—Vietnamese and Lao guys mostly. "Whatever their families did or ate, i did and ate too. We ate a lot of tiet canh."

Thanksgiving, 10 Years ago.

And there's the kickoff!

Damn, I want tiet canh. Let's make tiet Canh.

Right. How are we supposed to get duck blood?

CLOSED

CLOSED

What about the park?

Nobody will be there.

We'll just take one or two.

And how's that going to work?

"It's like catching minnows for fishing bait."

"You drive them into the center and then throw a net over them..."

Then you slice the throat of a live duck and collect the fresh blood.

Mix the blood with salt, fish sauce, and sugar, and let it sit in a cooler until it gelatinizes.

Eat it with coconut chips, chilies, lime juice, and fresh herbs. It is drinking food.

Chop up the duck meat. Cook it and mix it with herbs, like a larb salad.

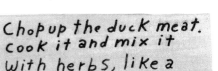

When the blood is set, garnish the meat with it.

The second half is about to get underway.

I look back and I can't believe we did that. Sometimes we still go fishing at that park, but we'd never take a duck again.

Want to see your kitchen tales told in comic form?

email us:
cooklife
@LKY.PH

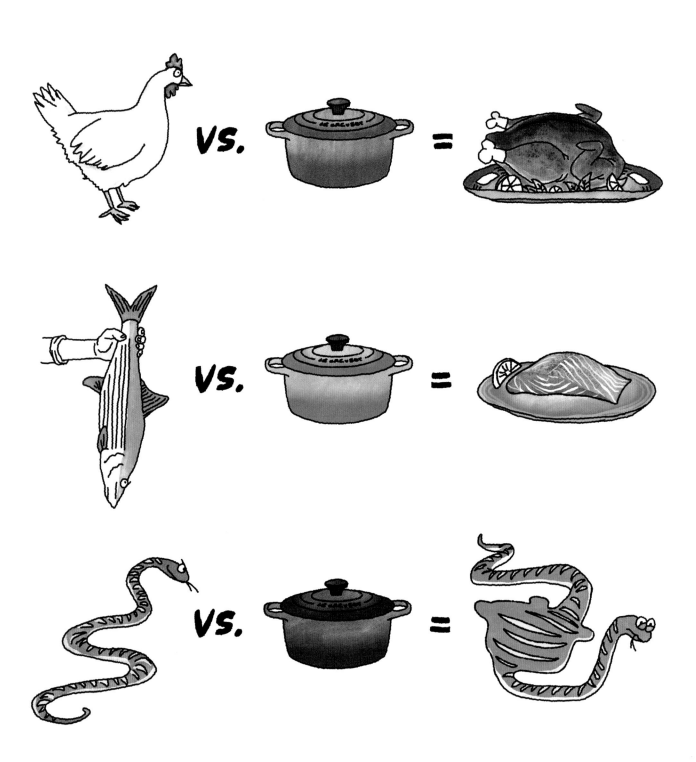

VIRTUALLY UNDEFEATED SINCE 1925.

LECREUSET.COM

CONTRIBUTORS

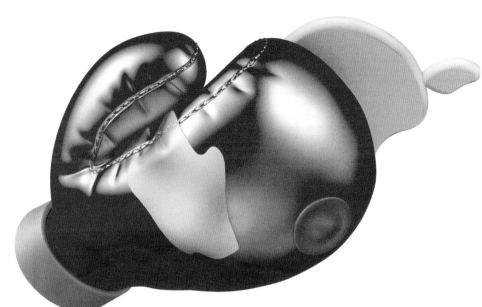

JOHN BIRDSALL writes about food and places. Previous stories in *Lucky Peach* have been about the gay roots of modern American food, cooking with rotting ingredients at a hardcore monastery, and this weird *pibil* in the Yucatán. Follow him on Twitter @John_Birdsall.

MARK BITTMAN is one of America's best-known, most beloved and widely respected food writers. He covered food policy as an opinion columnist for the *New York Times* for over four years, produced "The Minimalist" column for over thirteen years, and has starred in several popular television series, including the Emmy-winning *Years of Living Dangerously*. He recently left the *Times* to devote his time to cookbooks, teaching at UC Berkeley, and working on food-movement strategy with the Union of Concerned Scientists. He also cofounded Purple Carrot, a national company that delivers weekly vegan meal kits. Bittman has authored more than a dozen cookbooks, including the best-selling *How to Cook Everything, How to Cook Every-thing The Basics, How to Cook Everything Vegetarian* (all available as apps), *How to Cook Everything Fast, Food Matters,* and *VB6: Eat Vegan Before 6:00.*

DARK IGLOO is a company that specializes.

ELEANOR DAVIS is a cartoonist and illustrator from Tucson, Arizona. She now lives in Athens, Georgia.

PETE DEVAKUL spent the beginning of 2012 trying to get three questions answered by Rikrit Tiravanija for *White Zinfandel* magazine. His recent book *ENERGY* is about stimulant-infused cocktails.

CALVIN GODFREY is a writer and photographer based in Ho Chi Minh City. Hire him for general fixing or to take you and yours on a gluttonous marathon of street food and foot massages, at *savorsaigon.com*.

AMELIA GRAY is the author of four books: *AM/PM, Museum of the Weird, THREATS,*

WALTER GREEN is a graphic designer based in San Francisco. [Ed. Note: He used to be the art director of this magazine.]

BRIDGET HUBER is a writer and radio producer in Berkeley, California.

ROWAN JACOBSEN is the author of *American Terroir, Apples of Uncommon Character,* and other books. His newest book, *The Essential Oyster,* will be released in the fall.

and *Gutshot*. Her fiction and essays have appeared in the *New Yorker,* the *New York Times,* the *Wall Street Journal, Tin House,* and *Vice.* She lives in Los Angeles.

Award-winning food writer **ROBERT SIETSEMA** has inspired generations to explore the wealth of dining options across the five boroughs of New York City. The restaurant critic for the *Village Voice* from 1993 to 2013, and a current restaurant critic at Eater, he is also the author of *New York in a Dozen Dishes.*

MICHAEL SNYDER is a freelance journalist based in Mumbai, writing about food, culture, travel, and miscellanea His work has appeared in *T Magazine, Saveur, Vice, Travel + Leisure,* and the *New York Times,* among others.

DAN STAFFORD is an illustrator from London, working with editorial clients such as the *New York Times,* the *Guardian,* and *Bloomberg Businessweek.* He is also the editor and creator of *Amuseum,* the playful magazine that sees objects differently.

BRECHT VANDENBROUCKE is a Belgian cartoonist and illustrator. Since graduating from art school a few years ago, he has worked for numerous periodicals and the *New York Times* and has participated in group shows all over the world. His first solo exhibition took place in 2013.

MATTHEW VOLZ works on painting, illustration, and video projects. He travels doing stage and light design for Uruguayan musician and frequent collaborator Juan Wauters. He lives in Far Rockaway, Queens, where he is currently working on an illustrated book called *Brother.*

CHRIS VON AMELN is an artist and photographer born in São Paulo. He's collaborated with several magazines and newspapers, such as *Folha de S.Paulo, O Estado de S. Paulo, Agência Fotosite,* and *Joyce Pascowitch* magazine, among others. He lives in São Paulo, where he develops visual arts, mainly on printing techniques and painting.

ALICE MOLONEY is a London-based creative at INT Works, the sister agency of It's Nice That, where she combines drawing with research, design, and strategy. Alongside this, she is a freelance illustrator for clients such as the *Guardian* and the *Sunday Times Magazine.*

KEVIN PANG spent this past decade writing about food for the *Chicago Tribune.*

LUCAS PETERSON lives in Los Angeles but is from the great state of Illinois. He's a JBFA nominee, hosts *Dining on a Dime* on Eater, was once the keyboardist for a boy band called Big Time Rush, and is a two-time *Jeopardy!* champion.

JACK SACHS is an illustrator/animator from South London. A 2013 graduate of Camberwell College of Arts, Jack uses 3-D software and his bare hands to create strange and lumpy worlds.

CHRISTIAN SCHUBERT is an illustrator from London. He loves color, appreciates weird things, and has never eaten a scallop.

TAMARA SHOPSIN is a graphic designer and illustrator whose work is regularly featured in the *New York Times* and the *New Yorker.* She is the author of the memoir *Mumbai New York Scranton,* creator of the children's book *What Is This?,* and designer of the *5 Year Diary.* She is also a cook at her family's restaurant, Shopsin's, in New York.

MADHUR JAFFREY, actress and writer, is the winner of seven James Beard Awards, the Bert Greene Award for Food Journalism from the IACP, and the Silver Bear for Best Actress from the Berlin International Film Festival. Her first cookbook has also been inducted into the James Beard Hall of Fame and won the Culinary Classics Book Award from IACP.

JONATHAN KAUFFMAN is now a reporter with the *San Francisco Chronicle* after reviewing restaurants in the Bay Area and Seattle for more than a decade. Full disclosure: he does love a good beet-and-walnut salad.

ADAM KUBAN was the founder of *Slice,* the Internet's first pizza blog, and has been writing about pizza for twelve years. He ate pizza for lunch today and yesterday and probably the day before.

PATRICK KYLE is a multidisciplinary artist from Toronto. His third graphic novel, *Don't Come in Here,* will be released by Koyama Press later this year.

JULES LE BARAZER is a French illustrator living in Paris. Bodily fluids, tic disorders, and animal behavior are the sorts of things he gets his inspiration from.

ANDRIA LO is a freelance photographer who grew up in Alaska and Texas before moving to the Bay Area to study art. She never left and currently lives in Berkeley, California.

SAM LYON is an artist based in Dundee, Scotland.

JOSÉ MANDOJANA, a Seattle-based photographer, contributes regularly to *Wired, ESPN, Sunset, GQ, Men's Journal, Bloomberg Businessweek, Runner's World,* and *Dwell.* When he's not creating portraits, travel images, and advertising, in New York.

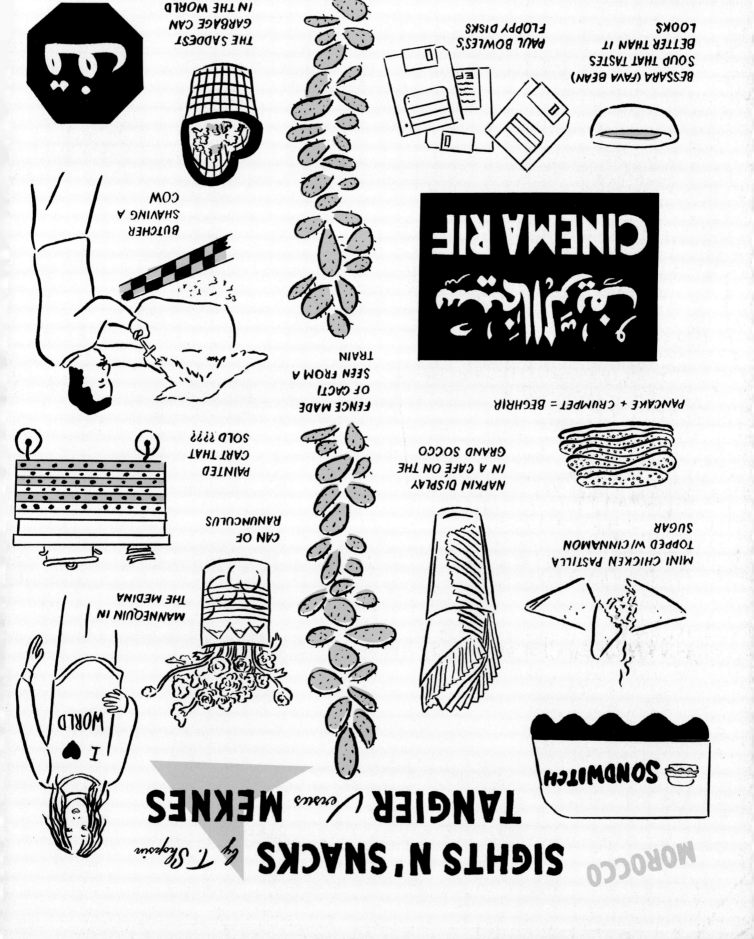